The Wyoming Ranch Letters

The Wyoming Ranch Letters
The Collected Correspondence of a
Woman Settler on the American Frontier

Letters of a Woman Homesteader

and

Letters On an Elk Hunt

Elinore Pruitt Stewart

LEONAUR

The Wyoming Ranch Letters
The Collected Correspondence of a Woman Settler on the American Frontier
Letters of a Woman Homesteader
and
Letters On an Elk Hunt
by Elinore Pruitt Stewart

FIRST EDITION

First published under the titles
Letters of a Woman Homesteader
and
Letters On an Elk Hunt

Leonaur is an imprint
of Oakpast Ltd

ISBN: 978-1-78282-253-0 (hardcover)
ISBN: 978-1-78282-254-7 (softcover)

http://www.leonaur.com

Publisher's Notes

The views expressed in this book are not necessarily
those of the publisher.

Contents

Letters of a Woman Homesteader

The Woman Homesteader

Contents

Original Publishers' Note

The writer of the following letters is a young woman who lost her husband in a railroad accident and went to Denver to seek support for herself and her two-year-old daughter, Jerrine. Turning her hand to the nearest work, she went out by the day as house-cleaner and laundress. Later, seeking to better herself, she accepted employment as a housekeeper for a well-to-do Scotch cattle-man, Mr. Stewart, who had taken up a quarter-section in Wyoming. The letters, written through several years to a former employer in Denver, tell the story of her new life in the new country. They are genuine letters, and are printed as written, except for occasional omissions and the alteration of some of the names.

1

The Arrival at Burnt Fork

Burnt Fork, Wyoming,
April 18, 1909.

Dear Mrs. Coney,—

Are you thinking I am lost, like the Babes in the Wood? Well, I am not and I'm sure the robins would have the time of their lives getting leaves to cover me out here. I am 'way up close to the Forest Reserve of Utah, within half a mile of the line, sixty miles from the railroad. I was twenty-four hours on the train and two days on the stage, and oh, those two days! The snow was just beginning to melt and the mud was about the worst I ever heard of.

The first stage we tackled was just about as rickety as it could very well be and I had to sit with the driver, who was a Mormon and so handsome that I was not a bit offended when he insisted on making love all the way, especially after he told me that he was a widower Mormon. But, of course, as I had no chaperone I looked very fierce (not that that was very difficult with the wind and mud as allies) and told him my actual opinion of Mormons in general and particular.

Meantime my new employer, Mr. Stewart, sat upon a stack of baggage and was dreadfully concerned about something he calls his "Tookie," but I am unable to tell you what that is. The road, being so muddy, was full of ruts and the stage acted as if it had the hiccoughs and made us all talk as though we were affected in the same way. Once Mr. Stewart asked me if I did not think it a "gey duir trip." I told him he could call it gay if he wanted to, but it didn't seem very hilarious to me. Every time the stage struck a rock or a rut Mr. Stewart would "hoot," until I began to wish we would come to a hollow tree or a hole in the ground so he could go in with the rest of the owls.

At last we "arriv," and everything is just lovely for me. I have a very,

very comfortable situation and Mr. Stewart is absolutely no trouble, for as soon as he has his meals he retires to his room and plays on his bagpipe, only he calls it his "bugpeep." It is "The Campbells are Coming," without variations, at intervals all day long and from seven till eleven at night. Sometimes I wish they would make haste and get here.

There is a saddle horse especially for me and a little shotgun with which I am to kill sage chickens. We are between two trout streams, so you can think of me as being happy when the snow is through melting and the water gets clear. We have the finest flock of Plymouth Rocks and get so many nice eggs. It sure seems fine to have all the cream I want after my town experiences. Jerrine is making good use of all the good things we are having. She rides the pony to water every day.

I have not filed on my land yet because the snow is fifteen feet deep on it, and I think I would rather see what I am getting, so will wait until summer. They have just three seasons here, winter and July and August. We are to plant our garden the last of May. When it is so I can get around I will see about land and find out all I can and tell you.

I think this letter is about to reach thirty-secondly, so I will send you my sincerest love and quit tiring you. Please write me when you have time.

Sincerely yours,

Elinore Rupert.

2

Filing a Claim

Dear, dear Mrs. Coney,—

Well, I have filed on my land and am now a bloated landowner. I waited a long time to even *see* land in the reserve, and the snow is yet too deep, so I thought that as they have but three months of summer and spring together and as I wanted the land for a ranch anyway, perhaps I had better stay in the valley. So I have filed adjoining Mr. Stewart and I am well pleased. I have a grove of twelve swamp pines on my place, and I am going to build my house there. I thought it would be very romantic to live on the peaks amid the whispering pines, but I reckon it would be powerfully uncomfortable also, and I guess my twelve can whisper enough for me; and a dandy thing is, I have all the nice snow-water I want; a small stream runs right through the centre of my land and I am quite near wood.

A neighbour and his daughter were going to Green River, the county-seat, and said I might go along, so I did, as I could file there as well as at the land office; and oh, that trip! I had more fun to the square inch than Mark Twain or Samantha Allen *ever* provoked. It took us a whole week to go and come. We camped out, of course, for in the whole sixty miles there was but one house, and going in that direction there is not a tree to be seen, nothing but sage, sand, and sheep. About noon the first day out we came near a sheep-wagon, and stalking along ahead of us was a lanky fellow, a herder, going home for dinner. Suddenly it seemed to me I should starve if I had to wait until we got where we had planned to stop for dinner, so I called out to the man, "Little Bo-Peep, have you anything to eat? If you have, we'd like to find it." And he answered, "As soon as I am able it shall be on the table, if you'll but trouble to get behind it." Shades of Shakespeare! Songs

15

of David, the Shepherd Poet! What do you think of us? Well, we got behind it, and a more delicious "it" I never tasted. Such coffee! And out of *such* a pot! I promised Bo-Peep that I would send him a crook with pink ribbons on it, but I suspect he thinks I am a crook without the ribbons.

The sagebrush is so short in some places that it is not large enough to make a fire, so we had to drive until quite late before we camped that night. After driving all day over what seemed a level desert of sand, we came about sundown to a beautiful *cañon*, down which we had to drive for a couple of miles before we could cross. In the *cañon* the shadows had already fallen, but when we looked up we could see the last shafts of sunlight on the tops of the great bare buttes. Suddenly a great wolf started from somewhere and galloped along the edge of the *cañon*, outlined black and clear by the setting sun. His curiosity overcame him at last, so he sat down and waited to see what manner of beast we were. I reckon he was disappointed for he howled most dismally. I thought of Jack London's "The Wolf."

After we quitted the *cañon* I saw the most beautiful sight. It seemed as if we were driving through a golden haze. The violet shadows were creeping up between the hills, while away back of us the snow-capped peaks were catching the sun's last rays. On every side of us stretched the poor, hopeless desert, the sage, grim and determined to live in spite of starvation, and the great, bare, desolate buttes. The beautiful colours turned to amber and rose, and then to the general tone, dull gray. Then we stopped to camp, and such a scurrying around to gather brush for the fire and to get supper! Everything tasted so good! Jerrine ate like a man. Then we raised the wagon tongue and spread the wagon sheet over it and made a bedroom for us women. We made our beds on the warm, soft sand and went to bed.

It was too beautiful a night to sleep, so I put my head out to look and to think. I saw the moon come up and hang for a while over the mountain as if it were discouraged with the prospect, and the big white stars flirted shamelessly with the hills. I saw a coyote come trotting along and I felt sorry for him, having to hunt food in so barren a place, but when presently I heard the whirr of wings I felt sorry for the sage chickens he had disturbed. At length a cloud came up and I went to sleep, and next morning was covered several inches with snow. It didn't hurt us a bit, but while I was struggling with stubborn corsets and shoes I communed with myself, after the manner of prodigals, and said: "How much better that I were down in Denver, even at Mrs.

Coney's, digging with a skewer into the corners seeking dirt which *might* be there, yea, even eating codfish, than that I should perish on this desert—of imagination." So I turned the current of my imagination and fancied that I was at home before the fireplace, and that the backlog was about to roll down. My fancy was in such good working trim that before I knew it I kicked the wagon wheel, and I certainly got as warm as the most "sot" Scientist that ever read Mrs. Eddy could possibly wish.

After two more such days I "arrived." When I went up to the office where I was to file, the door was open and the most taciturn old man sat before a desk. I hesitated at the door, but he never let on. I coughed, yet no sign but a deeper scowl. I stepped in and modestly kicked over a chair. He whirled around like I had shot him.

"Well?" he interrogated.

I said, "I am powerful glad of it. I was afraid you were sick, you looked in such pain." He looked at me a minute, then grinned and said he thought I was a book-agent. Fancy me, a fat, comfortable widow, trying to sell books!

Well, I filed and came home. If you will believe me, the Scot was glad to see me and didn't herald the Campbells for two hours after I got home. I'll tell you, it is mighty seldom anyone's so much appreciated.

No, we have no rural delivery. It is two miles to the office, but I go whenever I like. It is really the jolliest kind of fun to gallop down. We are sixty miles from the railroad, but when we want anything we send by the mail-carrier for it, only there is nothing to get.

I know this is an inexcusably long letter, but it is snowing so hard and you know how I like to talk. I am sure Jerrine will enjoy the cards and we will be glad to get them. Many things that are a comfort to us out here came from dear Mrs. ——. Baby has the rabbit you gave her last Easter a year ago. In Denver I was afraid my baby would grow up devoid of imagination. Like all the kindergartners, she depended upon others to amuse her. I was very sorry about it, for my castles in Spain have been real homes to me. But there is no fear. She has a block of wood she found in the blacksmith shop which she calls her "dear baby." A spoke out of a wagon wheel is "little Margaret," and a barrel-stave is "bad little Johnny."

Well, I must quit writing before you vote me a nuisance. With lots of love to you,

Your sincere friend,

Elinore Rupert.

3

A Busy, Happy Summer

September 11, 1909.

Dear Mrs. Coney,—

This has been for me the busiest, happiest summer I can remember. I have worked very hard, but it has been work that I really enjoy. Help of any kind is very hard to get here, and Mr. Stewart had been too confident of getting men, so that haying caught him with too few men to put up the hay. He had no man to run the mower and he couldn't run both the mower and the stacker, so you can fancy what a place he was in.

I don't know that I ever told you, but my parents died within a year of each other and left six of us to shift for ourselves. Our people offered to take one here and there among them until we should all have a place, but we refused to be raised on the halves and so arranged to stay at Grandmother's and keep together. Well, we had no money to hire men to do our work, so had to learn to do it ourselves. Consequently I learned to do many things which girls more fortunately situated don't even know have to be done. Among the things I learned to do was the way to run a mowing-machine. It cost me many bitter tears because I got sunburned, and my hands were hard, rough, and stained with machine oil, and I used to wonder how any Prince Charming could overlook all that in any girl he came to. For all I had ever read of the prince had to do with his "reverently kissing her lily-white hand," or doing some other fool trick with a hand as white as a snowflake.

Well, when my prince showed up he didn't lose much time in letting me know that "*Barkis was willing,*" and I wrapped my hands in my old checked apron and took him up before he could catch his breath. Then there was no more mowing, and I almost forgot that I knew how until Mr. Stewart got into such a panic. If he put a man to mow, it kept them all idle at the stacker, and he just couldn't get enough men. I was afraid to tell him I could mow for fear he would forbid me to do so. But one morning, when he was chasing a last hope of help, I went down to the barn, took out the horses, and went to mowing. I had enough cut before he got back to show him I knew how, and as he came back manless he was delighted as well as surprised. I was glad because I really like to mow, and besides that, I am adding feathers to my cap in a surprising way. When you see me again you will think I am wearing a feather duster, but it is only that I have been said to have almost as much sense as a "mon," and that is an honour I never aspired to, even in my wildest dreams.

I have done most of my cooking at night, have milked seven cows every day, and have done all the hay-cutting, so you see I have been working. But I have found time to put up thirty pints of jelly and the same amount of jam for myself. I used wild fruits, gooseberries, currants, raspberries, and cherries. I have almost two gallons of the cherry butter, and I think it is delicious. I wish I could get some of it to you, I am sure you would like it.

We began haying July 5 and finished September 8. After working so hard and so steadily I decided on a day off, so yesterday I saddled the pony, took a few things I needed, and Jerrine and I fared forth. Baby can ride behind quite well. We got away by sunup and a glorious day we had. We followed a stream higher up into the mountains and the air was so keen and clear at first we had on our coats. There was a tang of sage and of pine in the air, and our horse was midside deep in rabbit-brush, a shrub just covered with flowers that look and smell like goldenrod. The blue distance promised many alluring adventures, so we went along singing and simply gulping in summer. Occasionally a bunch of sage chickens would fly up out of the sagebrush, or a jack rabbit would leap out. Once we saw a bunch of antelope gallop over a hill, but we were out just to be out, and game didn't tempt us. I started, though, to have just as good a time as possible, so I had a fish-hook in my knapsack.

Presently, about noon, we came to a little dell where the grass was as soft and as green as a lawn. The creek kept right up against the hills on one side and there were groves of quaking asp and cottonwoods that made shade, and service-bushes and birches that shut off the ugly hills on the other side. We dismounted and prepared to noon. We caught a few grasshoppers and I cut a birch pole for a rod. The trout are so beautiful now, their sides are so silvery, with dashes of old rose and orange, their speckles are so black, while their backs look as if they had been sprinkled with gold-dust. They bite so well that it doesn't require any especial skill or tackle to catch plenty for a meal in a few minutes.

In a little while I went back to where I had left my pony browsing, with eight beauties. We made a fire first, then I dressed my trout while it was burning down to a nice bed of coals. I had brought a frying-pan and a bottle of lard, salt, and buttered bread. We gathered a few service-berries, our trout were soon browned, and with water, clear, and as cold as ice, we had a feast. The quaking aspens are beginning to turn yellow, but no leaves have fallen. Their shadows dimpled and twinkled over the grass like happy children. The sound of the dashing, roaring water kept inviting me to cast for trout, but I didn't want to carry them so far, so we rested until the sun was getting low and then started for home, with the song of the locusts in our ears warning us that the melancholy days are almost here. We would come up over the top of a hill into the glory of a beautiful sunset with its gorgeous colours, then down into the little valley already purpling with mysterious twilight. So on, until, just at dark, we rode into our corral and a mighty tired, sleepy little girl was powerfully glad to get home.

After I had mailed my other letter I was afraid that you would think me plumb bold about the little Bo-Peep, and was a heap sorrier than you can think. If you only knew the hardships these poor men endure. They go two together and sometimes it is months before they see another soul, and rarely ever a woman. I wouldn't act so free in town, but these men see people so seldom that they are awkward and embarrassed. I like to put them at ease, and it is to be done only by being kind of hail-fellow-well-met with them. So far not one has ever misunderstood me and I have been treated with every courtesy and kindness, so I am powerfully glad you understand. They really enjoy doing these little things like fixing our dinner, and if my poor company can add to anyone's pleasure I am too glad.

Sincerely yours,

Elinore Rupert.

Mr. Stewart is going to put up my house for me in pay for my extra work.

I am ashamed of my long letters to you, but I am such a murderer of language that I have to use it all to tell anything.

Please don't entirely forget me. Your letters mean so much to me and I will try to answer more promptly.

4

A Charming Adventure and Zebulon Pike

September 28, 1909.

Dear Mrs. Coney,—

Your second card just reached me and I am plumb glad because, although I answered your other, I was wishing I could write you, for I have had the most charming adventure.

It is the custom here for as many women as care to to go in a party over into Utah to Ashland (which is over a hundred miles away) after fruit. They usually go in September, and it takes a week to make the trip. They take wagons and camp out and of course have a good time, but, the greater part of the way, there isn't even the semblance of a road and it is merely a semblance anywhere. They came over to invite me to join them. I was of two minds—I wanted to go, but it seemed a little risky and a big chance for discomfort, since we would have to cross the Uinta Mountains, and a snowstorm likely any time. But I didn't like to refuse outright, so we left it to Mr. Stewart. His "Ye're nae gang" sounded powerful final, so the ladies departed in awed silence and I assumed a martyr-like air and acted like a very much abused woman, although he did only what I wanted him to do.

At last, in sheer desperation he told me the "bairn canna stand the treep," and that was why he was so determined. I knew why, of course, but I continued to look abused lest he gets it into his head that he can boss me. After he had been reduced to the proper plane of humility and had explained and begged my pardon and had told me to consult only my own pleasure about going and coming and using his horses, only not to "expose" the bairn, why, I forgave him and we were friends once more.

Next day all the men left for the roundup, to be gone a week. I knew I never could stand myself a whole week. In a little while the ladies came past on their way to Ashland. They were all laughing and were so happy that I really began to wish I was one of the number, but they went their way and I kept wanting to go *somewhere*. I got reckless and determined to do something real bad. So I went down to the barn and saddled Robin Adair, placed a pack on "Jeems McGregor," then Jerrine and I left for a camping-out expedition.

It was nine o'clock when we started and we rode hard until about four, when I turned Robin loose, saddle and all, for I knew he would go home and someone would see him and put him into the pasture. We had gotten to where we couldn't ride anyway, so I put Jerrine on the pack and led "Jeems" for about two hours longer; then, as I had come to a good place to camp, we stopped.

While we had at least two good hours of daylight, it gets so cold here in the evening that fire is very necessary. We had been climbing higher into the mountains all day and had reached a level tableland where the grass was luxuriant and there was plenty of wood and water. I unpacked "Jeems" and staked him out, built a roaring fire, and made our bed in an angle of a sheer wall of rock where we would be protected against the wind. Then I put some potatoes into the embers, as baby and I are both fond of roasted potatoes. I started to a little spring to get water for my coffee when I saw a couple of jack rabbits playing, so I went back for my little shotgun. I shot one of the rabbits, so I felt very like Leather-stocking because I had killed but one when I might have gotten two. It was fat and young, and it was but the work of a moment to dress it and hang it up on a tree. Then I fried some slices of bacon, made myself a cup of coffee, and Jerrine and I sat on the ground and ate. Everything smelled and tasted so good! This air is so tonic that one gets delightfully hungry. Afterward we watered and restaked "Jeems," I rolled some logs on to the fire, and then we sat and enjoyed the prospect.

The moon was so new that its light was very dim, but the stars were bright. Presently a long, quivering wail arose and was answered from a dozen hills. It seemed just the sound one ought to hear in such a place. When the howls ceased for a moment we could hear the subdued roar of the creek and the crooning of the wind in the pines. So we rather enjoyed the coyote chorus and were not afraid, because they don't attack people. Presently we crept under our Navajos and, being tired, were soon asleep.

I was awakened by a pebble striking my cheek. Something prowling on the bluff above us had dislodged it and it struck me. By my Waterbury it was four o'clock, so I arose and spitted my rabbit. The logs had left a big bed of coals, but some ends were still burning and had burned in such a manner that the heat would go both under and over my rabbit. So I put plenty of bacon grease over him and hung him up to roast. Then I went back to bed. I didn't want to start early because the air is too keen for comfort early in the morning.

The sun was just gilding the hilltops when we arose. Everything, even the barrenness, was beautiful. We have had frosts, and the quaking aspens were a trembling field of gold as far up the stream as we could see. We were 'way up above them and could look far across the valley. We could see the silvery gold of the willows, the russet and bronze of the currants, and patches of cheerful green showed where the pines were. The splendor was relieved by a background of sober gray-green hills, but even on them gay streaks and patches of yellow showed where rabbit-brush grew. We washed our faces at the spring,—the grasses that grew around the edge and dipped into the water were loaded with ice,—our rabbit was done to a turn, so I made some delicious coffee, Jerrine got herself a can of water, and we breakfasted. Shortly afterwards we started again. We didn't know where we were going, but we were on our way.

That day was more toilsome than the last, but a very happy one. The meadowlarks kept singing like they were glad to see us. But we were still climbing and soon got beyond the larks and sage chickens and up into the timber, where there are lots of grouse. We stopped to noon by a little lake, where I got two small squirrels and a string of trout. We had some trout for dinner and salted the rest with the squirrels in an empty can for future use. I was anxious to get a grouse and kept close watch, but was never quick enough. Our progress was now slower and more difficult, because in places we could scarcely get through the forest. Fallen trees were everywhere and we had to avoid the branches, which was powerful hard to do. Besides, it was quite dusky among the trees long before night, but it was all so grand and awe-inspiring.

Occasionally there was an opening through which we could see the snowy peaks, seemingly just beyond us, toward which we were headed. But when you get among such grandeur you get to feel how little you are and how foolish is human endeavor, except that which reunites us with the mighty force called God. I was plumb uncom-

JERRINE WAS ALWAYS SUCH A DEAR LITTLE PAL.

fortable, because all my own efforts have always been just to make the best of everything and to take things as they come.

At last we came to an open side of the mountain where the trees were scattered. We were facing south and east, and the mountain we were on sheered away in a dangerous slant. Beyond us still greater wooded mountains blocked the way, and in the *cañon* between night had already fallen. I began to get scary. I could only think of bears and catamounts, so, as it was five o'clock, we decided to camp. The trees were immense. The lower branches came clear to the ground and grew so dense that any tree afforded a splendid shelter from the weather, but I was nervous and wanted one that would protect us against any possible attack.

At last we found one growing in a crevice of what seemed to be a sheer wall of rock. Nothing could reach us on two sides, and in front two large trees had fallen so that I could make a log heap which would give us warmth and make us safe. So with rising spirits I unpacked and prepared for the night. I soon had a roaring fire up against the logs and, cutting away a few branches, let the heat into as snug a bedroom as anyone could wish. The pine needles made as soft a carpet as the wealthiest could afford. Springs abound in the mountains, so water was plenty. I staked "Jeems" quite near so that the firelight would frighten away any wild thing that tried to harm him.

Grass was very plentiful, so when he was made "comfy" I made our bed and fried our trout. The branches had torn off the bag in which I had my bread, so it was lost in the forest, but who needs bread when they have good, mealy potatoes? In a short time we were eating like Lent was just over. We lost all the glory of the sunset except what we got by reflection, being on the side of the mountain we were, with the dense woods between. Big sullen clouds kept drifting over and a wind got lost in the trees that kept them rocking and groaning in a horrid way. But we were just as cosy as we could be and rest was as good as anything.

I wish you could once sleep on the kind of bed we enjoyed that night. It was both soft and firm, with the clean, spicy smell of the pine. The heat from our big fire came in and we were warm as toast. It was so good to stretch out and rest. I kept thinking how superior I was since I dared to take such an outing when so many poor women down in Denver were bent on making their twenty cents per hour in order that they could spare a quarter to go to the "show." I went to sleep with a powerfully self-satisfied feeling, but I awoke to realise that *pride goeth before a fall.*

I could hardly remember where I was when I awoke, and I could almost hear the silence. Not a tree moaned, not a branch seemed to stir. I arose and my head came in violent contact with a snag that was not there when I went to bed. I thought either I must have grown taller or the tree shorter during the night. As soon as I peered out, the mystery was explained.

Such a snowstorm I never saw! The snow had pressed the branches down lower, hence my bumped head. Our fire was burning merrily and the heat kept the snow from in front. I scrambled out and poked up the fire; then, as it was only five o'clock, I went back to bed. And then I began to think how many kinds of idiot I was. Here I was thirty or forty miles from home, in the mountains where no one goes in the winter and where I knew the snow got to be ten or fifteen feet deep. But I could never see the good of moping, so I got up and got breakfast while Baby put her shoes on. We had our squirrels and more baked potatoes and I had delicious black coffee.

After I had eaten I felt more hopeful. I knew Mr. Stewart would hunt for me if he knew I was lost. It was true, he wouldn't know which way to start, but I determined to rig up "Jeems" and turn him loose, for I knew he would go home and that he would leave a trail so that I could be found. I hated to do so, for I knew I should always have to be powerfully humble afterwards. Anyway it was still snowing, great, heavy flakes; they looked as large as dollars. I didn't want to start "Jeems" until the snow stopped because I wanted him to leave a clear trail. I had sixteen loads for my gun and I reasoned that I could likely kill enough food to last twice that many days by being careful what I shot at.

It just kept snowing, so at last I decided to take a little hunt and provide for the day. I left Jerrine happy with the towel rolled into a baby, and went along the brow of the mountain for almost a mile, but the snow fell so thickly that I couldn't see far. Then I happened to look down into the *cañon* that lay east of us and saw smoke. I looked toward it a long time, but could make out nothing but smoke, but presently I heard a dog bark and I knew I was near a camp of some kind. I resolved to join them, so went back to break my own camp.

At last everything was ready and Jerrine and I both mounted. Of all the times! If you think there is much comfort, or even security, in riding a pack-horse in a snowstorm over mountains where there is no road, you are plumb wrong. Every once in a while a tree would unload its snow down our backs. "Jeems" kept stumbling and threatening to break our necks. At last we got down the mountain-side, where new danger confronted us,—we might lose sight of the smoke or ride into a bog. But at last, after what seemed hours, we came into a "clearing" with a small log house and, what is rare in Wyoming, a fireplace. Three or four hounds set up their deep baying, and I knew by the chimney and the hounds that it was the home of a Southerner. A little old man came bustling out, chewing his tobacco so fast, and almost frantic about his suspenders, which it seemed he couldn't get adjusted.

As I rode up, he said, "Whither, friend?"

I said "Hither."

Then he asked, "Air you spying around for one of them dinged game wardens arter that deer I killed yisteddy?" I told him I had never even seen a game warden and that I didn't know he had killed a deer. "Wall," he said, "air you spying around arter that gold mine I dis-kivered over on the west side of Baldy?" But after a while I convinced him that I was no more nor less than a foolish woman lost in the snow. Then he said, "Light, stranger, and look at your saddle."

So I "lit" and looked, and then I asked him what part of the South he was from. He answered, "Yell County, by gum! The best place in the United States, or in the world, either." That was my introduction to Zebulon Pike Parker.

Only two "Johnny Rebs" could have enjoyed each other's company as Zebulon Pike and myself did. He was so small and so old, but so cheerful and so sprightly, and a real Southerner! He had a big, open fireplace with backlogs and and irons. How I enjoyed it all! How we feasted on some of the deer killed "yisteddy," and real corn-pone baked in a skillet down on the hearth. He was so full of happy recollections and had a few that were not so happy! He is, in some way, a kinsman of Pike of Pike's Peak fame, and he came west "jist arter the wah" on some expedition and "jist stayed." He told me about his home life back in Yell County, and I feel that I know all the "young uns."

There was George Henry, his only brother; and there were Phœbe and "Mothie," whose real name is Martha; and poor little Mary Ann, whose death was described so feelingly that no one could keep back the tears. Lastly there was little Mandy, the baby and his favourite, but who, I am afraid, was a selfish little beast since she had to have her prunellas when all the rest of the "young uns" had to wear shoes that old Uncle Buck made out of rawhide. But then "her eyes were blue

27

as morning-glories and her hair was jist like corn-silk, so yaller and fluffy." Bless his simple, honest heart! His own eyes are blue and kind, and his poor, thin little shoulders are so round that they almost meet in front. How he loved to talk of his boyhood days! I can almost see his father and George Henry as they marched away to the "wah" together, and the poor little mother's despair as she waited day after day for some word, that never came.

Poor little Mary Ann was drowned in the bayou, where she was trying to get water-lilies. She had wanted a white dress all her life and so, when she was dead, they took down the white cross-bar curtains and Mother made the little shroud by the light of a tallow dip. But, being made by hand, it took all the next day, too, so that they buried her by moonlight down back of the orchard under the big elm where the children had always had their swing. And they lined and covered her grave with big, fragrant water-lilies. As they lowered the poor little home-made coffin into the grave the mockingbirds began to sing and they sang all that dewy, moonlight night. Then little Mandy's wedding to Judge Carter's son Jim was described. She wore a "cream-colored poplin with a red rose throwed up in it," and the lace that was on Grandma's wedding dress. There were bowers of sweet Southern roses and honeysuckle and wistaria. Don't you know she was a dainty bride?

At last it came out that he had not heard from home since he left it. "Don't you ever write?" I asked.

"No, I am not an eddicated man, although I started to school. Yes'm, I started along of the rest, but they told me it was a Yankee teacher and I was 'fraid, so when I got most to the schoolhouse I hid in the bushes with my spelling-book, so that is all the learning I ever got. But my mother was an eddicated woman, yes'm, she could both read and write. I have the Bible she give me yit. Yes'm, you jist wait and I'll show you." After some rummaging in a box he came back with a small leather-bound Bible with print so small it was hard to read. After turning to the record of births and deaths he handed it to me, his wrinkled old face shining with pride as he said, "There, my mother wrote that with her own hand." I took the book and after a little deciphered that "Zebulon Pike Parker was born Feb. 10, 1830," written in the stiff, difficult style of long ago and written with poke-berry ink. He said his mother used to read about some "old feller that was jist covered with biles," so I read *Job* to him, and he was full of surprise they didn't "git some cherry bark and some sasparilly and bile it good and gin it to him."

He had a side room to his cabin, which was his bedroom; so that night he spread down a buffalo robe and two bearskins before the fire for Jerrine and me. After making sure there were no moths in them, I spread blankets over them and put a sleepy, happy little girl to bed, for he had insisted on making molasses candy for her because they happened to be born on the same day of the month. And then he played the fiddle until almost one o'clock. He played all the simple, sweet, old-time pieces, in rather a squeaky, jerky way, I am afraid, but the music suited the time and the place.

Next morning he called me early and when I went out I saw such a beautiful sunrise, well worth the effort of coming to see. I had thought his cabin in a *cañon*, but the snow had deceived me, for a few steps from the door the mountains seemed to drop down suddenly for several hundred feet and the first of the snow peaks seemed to lie right at our feet. Around its base is a great swamp, in which the swamp pines grow very thickly and from which a vapour was rising that got about halfway up the snow peak all around. Fancy to yourself a big jewel-box of dark green velvet lined with silver chiffon, the snow peak lying like an immense opal in its centre and over all the amber light of a new day. That is what it looked most like.

Well, we next went to the corral, where I was surprised to find about thirty head of sheep. Some of them looked like they should have been sold ten years before.

"Don't you ever sell any of your sheep?" I asked.

"No'm. There was a feller come here once and wanted to buy some of my wethers, but I wouldn't sell any because I didn't need any money." Then he went from animal to animal, caressing each and talking to them, calling them each by name. He milked his one cow, fed his two little mules, and then we went back to the house to cook breakfast. We had delicious venison steak, smoking hot, and hoe-cakes and the "bestest" coffee, and honey.

After breakfast we set out for home. Our pack transferred to one of the little mules, we rode "Jeems," and Mr. Parker rode the other mule. He took us another way, down *cañon* after *cañon*, so that we were able to ride all the time and could make better speed. We came down out of the snow and camped within twelve miles of home in an old, deserted ranch house. We had grouse and sage chicken for supper. I was so anxious to get home that I could hardly sleep, but at last I did and was only awakened by the odour of coffee, and barely had time to wash before Zebulon Pike called breakfast. Afterwards we fixed "Jeems's" pack so that I could still ride, for Zebulon Pike was very anxious to get back to his "critters."

Poor, lonely, childlike little man! He tried to tell me how glad he had been to entertain me. "Why," he said, "I was plumb glad to see you and right sorry to have you go. Why, I would jist as soon talk to you as to a nigger. Yes'm, I would. It has been almost as good as talking to old Aunt Dilsey." If a Yankee had said the same to me I would have demanded instant apology, but I know how the Southern heart longs for the dear, kindly old "niggers," so I came on homeward, thankful for the first time that I can't talk correctly.

I got home at twelve and found, to my joy, that none of the men had returned, so I am safe from their superiority for a while, at least.

With many apologies for this outrageous letter, I am

Your ex-Washlady,

Elinore Rupert.

5

Sedalia and Regalia

November 22, 1909.

My dear Friend,—

I was dreadfully afraid that my last letter was too much for you
and now I feel plumb guilty. I really don't know how to write you,
for I have to write so much to say so little, and now that my last letter
made you sick I almost wish so many things didn't happen to me, for I
always want to tell you. Many things have happened since I last wrote,
and Zebulon Pike is not done for by any means, but I guess I will tell
you my newest experience.

I am making a wedding dress. Don't grin; it isn't mine,—worse
luck! But I must begin at the beginning. Just after I wrote you before,
there came a terrific storm which made me appreciate indoor cosi-
ness, but as only Baby and I were at home I expected to be very lonely.
The snow was just whirling when I saw some one pass the window.
I opened the door and in came the dumpiest little woman and two
daughters. She asked me if I was "Mis' Rupit." I told her that she
had almost guessed it, and then she introduced herself. She said she
was "Mis' Lane," that she had heard there was a new stranger in the
country, so she had brought her twin girls, Sedalia and Regalia, to be
neighbourly. While they were taking off their many coats and wraps
it came out that they were from Linwood, thirty miles away. I was
powerful glad I had a pot roast and some baked beans.

After we had put the horses in the barn we had dinner and I heard
the story of the girls' odd names. The mother is one of those "comfy,"
fat little women who remain happy and bubbling with fun in spite
of hard knocks. I had already fallen in love with Regalia, she is so
jolly and unaffected, so fat and so plain. Sedalia has a veneer of most
uncomfortable refinement. She was shocked because Gale ate all the

roast she wanted, and if I had been very sensitive I would have been in tears, because I ate a helping more than Gale did.

But about the names. It seemed that "Mis' Lane" married quite young, was an orphan, and had no one to tell her things she should have known. She lived in Missouri, but about a year after her marriage the young couple started overland for the West. It was in November, and one night when they had reached the plains a real blue blizzard struck them. "Mis' Lane" had been in pain all day and soon she knew what was the matter. They were alone and it was a day's travel back to the last house. The team had given out and the wind and sleet were seeing which could do the most meanness. At last the poor man got a fire started and a wagon sheet stretched in such a manner that it kept off the sleet. He fixed a bed under the poor shelter and did all he could to keep the fire from blowing away, and there, a few hours later, a little girl baby was born. They melted sleet in the frying-pan to get water to wash it. "Mis' Lane" kept feeling no better fast, and about the time they got the poor baby dressed a second little one came.

That she told me herself is proof she didn't die, I guess, but it is right hard to believe she didn't. Luckily the fire lasted until the babies were dressed and the mother began to feel better, for there was no wood. Soon the wind stopped and the snow fell steadily. It was warmer, and the whole family snuggled up under the wagon sheet and slept.

Mr. Lane is a powerful good husband. He waited two whole days for his wife to gain strength before he resumed the journey, and on the third morning he actually carried her to the wagon. Just think of it! Could more be asked of any man?

Every turn of the wheels made poor "Mis' Lane" more homesick. Like Mrs. Wiggs of the Cabbage Patch, she had a taste for geographical names, and "Mis' Lane" is very loyal, so she wanted to call the little first-born "Missouri." Mr. Lane said she might, but that if she did he would call the other one "Arkansas." Sometimes homesickness would almost master her. She would hug up the little red baby and murmur "Missouri," and then daddy would growl playfully to "Arkansas." It went on that way for a long time and at last she remembered that Sedalia was in Missouri, so she felt glad and really named the older baby "Sedalia." But she could think of nothing to match the name and was in constant fear the father would name the other baby "Little Rock."

For three years poor Gale was just "t'other one." Then the Lanes went to Green River where some lodge was having a parade. They were watching the drill when a "bystander that was standing by" said something about the "fine regalia." Instantly "Mis' Lane" thought of her unnamed child; so since that time Gale has had a name.

There could be no two people more unlike than the sisters. Sedalia is really handsome, and she is thin. But she is vain, selfish, shallow, and conceited. Gale is not even pretty, but she is clean and she is honest. She does many little things that are not exactly polite, but she is good and true. They both went to the barn with me to milk. Gale tucked up her skirts and helped me. She said, "I just love a stable, with its hay and comfortable, contented cattle. I never go into one without thinking of the little baby Christ. I almost expect to see a little red baby in the straw every time I peek into a manger."

Sedalia answered, "Well, for Heaven's sake, get out of the stable to preach. Who wants to stand among these smelly cows all day?"

They stayed with us almost a week, and one day when Gale and I were milking she asked me to invite her to stay with me a month. She said to ask her mother, and left her mother and myself much together. But Sedalia stuck to her mother like a plaster and I just could not stand Sedalia a whole month. However, I was spared all embarrassment, for "Mis' Lane" asked me if I could not find work enough to keep Gale busy for a month or two. She went on to explain that Sedalia was expecting to be married and that Gale was so "common" she would really spoil the match. I was surprised and indignant, especially as Sedalia sat and listened so brazenly, so I said I thought Sedalia would need all the help she could get to get married and that I should be glad to have Gale visit me as long as she liked.

So Gale stayed on with me. One afternoon she had gone to the post-office when I saw Mr. Patterson ride up. He went into the bunk-house to wait until the men should come. Now, from something Gale had said I fancied that Bob Patterson must be the right man. I am afraid I am not very delicate about that kind of meddling, and while I had been given to understand that Patterson was the man Sedalia expected to marry, I didn't think any man would choose her if he could get Gale, so I called him. We had a long chat and he told me frankly he wanted Gale, but that she didn't care for him, and that they kept throwing "that danged Sedalia" at him. Then he begged my pardon for saying "danged," but I told him I approved of the word when applied to Sedalia, and broke the news to him that Gale was staying with me. He fairly beamed.

So that night I left Gale to wash dishes and Bob to help her while

I held Mr. Stewart a prisoner in the stable and questioned him regarding Patterson's prospects and habits. I found both all that need be, and told Mr. Stewart about my talk with Patterson, and he said, "Wooman, some day ye'll gang ploom daft." But he admitted he was glad it was the "bonny lassie, instead of the bony one." When we went to the house Mr. Stewart said, "Weel, when are you douchy bairns gangin' to the kirk?"

They left it to me, so I set Thanksgiving Day, and as there is no "kirk to gang to," we are going to have a justice of the peace and they are to be married here. We are going to have the dandiest dinner that I can cook, and Mr. Stewart went to town next day for the wedding dress, the gayest plaid outside of Caledonia. But Gale has lots of sense and is going to wear it. I have it almost finished, and while it doesn't look just like a Worth model, still it looks plumb good for me to have made. The boys are going up after Zebulon Pike, and Mr. Stewart is going after "Mis' Lane." Joy waves are radiating from this ranch and about Thanksgiving morning one will strike you.

With lots of love and happy wishes,

Your ex-Washlady,

Elinore Rupert.

6

A Thanksgiving-Day Wedding

Dear Mrs. Coney,—

. . . . I think everyone enjoyed our Thanksgiving programme except poor Gale. She was grieved, I verily believe, because Mr. Patterson is not Mormon and could not take Sedalia and herself also. I suppose it seemed odd to her to be unable to give way to Sedalia as she had always done.

I had cooked and cooked. Gale and Zebulon Pike both helped all they could. The wedding was to be at twelve o'clock, so at ten I hustled Gale into my room to dress. I had to lock the door to keep her in, and I divided my time between the last touches to my dinner and the finishing touches to Gale's toilet and receiving the people. The Lane party had not come yet, and I was scared to death lest Sedalia had had a tantrum and that Mr. Stewart would not get back in time. At last I left the people to take care of themselves, for I had too much on my mind to bother with them. Just after eleven Mr. Stewart, Mis' Lane, Sedalia, and Pa Lane "arriv" and came at once into the kitchen to warm. In a little while poor, frightened Gale came creeping in, looking guilty. But she looked lovely, too, in spite of her plaid dress. She wore her hair in a coronet braid, which added dignity and height, as well as being simple and becoming. Her mother brought her a wreath for her hair, of lilies of the valley and tiny pink rosebuds. It might seem a little out of place to one who didn't see it, but the effect was really charming.

Sedalia didn't know that Mr. Stewart had given Gale her dress, so, just to be nasty, she said, as soon as she saw Gale, "Dear me, when are you going to dress, Gale? You will hardly have time to get out of that horse-blanket you are wearing and get into something decent." You see, she thought it was one of my dresses fixed over for Gale. Presently Sedalia asked me if I was invited to the "function." She had some kind of rash on her face and Zebulon Pike noticed the rash and heard the word "function," so he thought that was the name of some disease and asked Mr. Stewart if the "function" was "catching." Mr. Stewart had heard Sedalia, but knew "Zebbie" had not heard all that was said and how he got the idea he had, so he answered, "Yes, if ye once get the fever." So Zebulon Pike privately warned every one against getting the "function" from Sedalia. There are plenty of people here who don't know exactly what a function is, myself among them. So people edged away from Sedalia, and some asked her if she had seen the doctor and what he thought of her case. Poor girl, I'm afraid she didn't have a very enjoyable time.

At last the "jestice" of the peace came, and I hope they live happy ever afterward. That night a dance was given to celebrate the event and we began to have dinner immediately after the wedding so as to get through in time to start, for dances are never given in the home here, but in "the hall." Every settlement has one and the invitations are merely written announcements posted everywhere. We have what Sedalia calls "homogenous" crowds. I wouldn't attempt to say what she means, but as everybody goes no doubt she is right.

Our dinner was a success, but that is not to be wondered at. Every woman for miles around contributed. Of course we had to borrow dishes, but we couldn't think of seating everyone; so we set one table for twenty-four and had three other long tables, on one of which we placed all the meats, pickles, and sauces, on another the vegetables, soup, and coffee, and on the third the pie, cakes, ice-cream, and other desserts. We had two big, long shelves, one above the other, on which were the dishes. The people helped themselves to dishes and neighbours took turns at serving from the tables, so people got what they wanted and hunted themselves a place to sit while they ate. Two of the cowboys from this ranch waited upon the table at which were the wedding party and some of their friends. Boys from other ranches helped serve and carried coffee, cake, and ice-cream.

The tablecloths were tolerably good linen and we had ironed them wet so they looked nice. We had white lace-paper on the shelves and we used drawn-work paper napkins. As I said, we borrowed dishes, or, that is, every woman who called herself our neighbour brought whatever she thought we would need. So after everyone had eaten I suggested that they sort out their dishes and wash them, and in that way I was saved all that work. We had everything done and were off to the dance by five o'clock. We went in sleds and sleighs, the snow was so deep, but it was all so jolly. Zebbie, Mr. Stewart, Jerrine, and I went in the bobsled. We jogged along at a comfortable pace lest the "beasties" should suffer, and every now and then a merry party would fly past us scattering snow in our faces and yelling like Comanches. We had a lovely moon then and the snow was so beautiful! We were driving northward, and to the south and back of us were the great sombre, pine-clad Uintah Mountains, while ahead and on every side were the bare buttes, looking like old men of the mountains,—so old they had lost all their hair, beard, and teeth.

7

Zebulon Pike Visits His Old Home

December 28, 1909.

Dear Mrs. Coney,—

Our Thanksgiving affair was the most enjoyable happening I can remember for a long time. Zebulon Pike came, but I had as a bait for him two fat letters from home. As soon as I came back from his place I wrote to Mrs. Carter and trusted to luck for my letter to reach her. I told her all I could about her brother and how seldom he left his mountain home. I asked her to write him all she could in one letter, as the trips between our place and his were so few and far between. So when she received my letter she wrote all she could think of, and then sent her letter and mine to Mothie and Phœbe, who are widows living in the old home. They each took turns writing, so their letters are a complete record of the years "Zebbie" has been gone. The letters were addressed to me along with a cordial letter from Mrs. Carter asking me to see that he got them and to use my judgment in the delivering. I couldn't go myself, but I wanted to read the letters to him and to write the answers; so I selected one piece of news I felt would bring him to hear the rest without his knowing how much there was for him.

Well, the boys brought him, and a more delighted little man I am sure never lived. I read the letters over and over, and answers were hurried off. He was dreadfully homesick, but couldn't figure on how he could leave the "critters," or how he could trust himself on a train. Mr. Stewart became interested, and he is a very resourceful man, so an old Frenchman was found who had no home and wanted a place to stay so he could trap. He was installed at Zebulon Pike's with full instructions as to each "critter's" peculiarities and needs. Then one of the boys, who was going home for Christmas to Memphis, was induced to wait for Mr. Parker and to see him safe to Little Rock. His money was banked for him, and Mr. Stewart saw that he was properly clothed and made comfortable for the trip. Then he sent a telegram to Judge Carter, who met Zebulon Pike at Little Rock, and they had a family reunion in Yell County. I have had some charming letters from there, but that only proves what I have always said, that I am the luckiest woman in finding really lovely people and having really happy experiences. Good things are constantly happening to me. I wish I could tell you about my happy Christmas, but one of my New Year's resolutions was to stop loading you down with two-thousand-word letters.

From something you wrote I think I must have written boastingly to you at some time. I have certainly not intended to, and you must please forgive me and remember how ignorant I am and how hard it is for me to express myself properly. I felt after I had written to Mr. Parker's people that I had taken a liberty, but luckily it was not thought of in that way by them. If you only knew how far short I fall of my own hopes you would know I could *never* boast. Why, it keeps me busy making over mistakes just like some one using old clothes. I get myself all ready to enjoy a success and find that I have to fit a failure. But one consolation is that I generally have plenty of material to cut generously, and many of my failures have proved to be real blessings.

I do hope this New Year may bring to you the desire of your heart and all that those who love you best most wish for you.

With lots and lots of love from baby and myself.

Your ex-washlady,

Elinore Rupert.

8

A Happy Christmas

Dear Mrs. Coney,—

My happy Christmas resulted from the ex-sheriff of this county being snowbound here. It seems that persons who come from a lower altitude to this country frequently become bewildered, especially if in poor health, leave the train at any stop and wander off into the hills, sometimes dying before they are found. The ex-sheriff cited a case, that of a young German who was returning from the Philippines, where he had been discharged after the war. He was the only child of his widowed mother, who has a ranch a few miles from here. No one knew he was coming home. One day the cook belonging to the camp of a construction gang went hunting and came back running, wild with horror. He had found the body of a man.

The coroner and the sheriff were notified, and next morning went out for the body, but the wolves had almost destroyed it. High up in a willow, under which the poor man had lain down to die, they saw a small bundle tied in a red bandanna and fast to a branch. They found a letter addressed to whoever should find it, saying that the body was that of Benny Louderer and giving them directions how to spare his poor old mother the awful knowledge of how he died. Also there was a letter to his mother asking her not to grieve for him and to keep their days faithfully. "Their days," I afterward learned, were anniversaries which they had always kept, to which was added "Benny's day."

Poor boy! When he realised that death was near his every thought was for the mother. Well, they followed his wishes, and the casket containing the bare, gnawed bones was sealed and never opened. And to this day poor Mrs. Louderer thinks her boy died of some fever while yet aboard the transport. The manner of his death has been kept so secret that I am the only one who has heard it.

I was so sorry for the poor mother that I resolved to visit her the first opportunity I had. I am at liberty to go where I please when there is no one to cook for. So, when the men left, a few days later, I took Jerrine and rode over to the Louderer ranch. I had never seen Mrs. Louderer and it happened to be "Benny's day" that I blundered in upon. I found her to be a dear old German woman living all alone, the people who do the work on the ranch living in another house two miles away. She had been weeping for hours when I got there, but in accordance with her custom on the many anniversaries, she had a real feast prepared, although no one had been bidden.

She says that God always sends her guests, but that was the first time she had had a little girl. She had a little daughter once herself, little Gretchen, but all that was left was a sweet memory and a pitifully small mound on the ranch, quite near the house, where Benny and Gretchen are at rest beside "*der fader, Herr Louderer.*"

She is such a dear old lady! She made us so welcome and she is so entertaining. All the remainder of the day we listened to stories of her children, looked at her pictures, and Jerrine had a lovely time with a wonderful wooden doll that they had brought with them from Germany. Mrs. Louderer forgot to weep in recalling her childhood days and showing us her treasures. And then our feast,—for it was verily a feast. We had goose and it was *so* delicious. I couldn't tell you half the good things any more than I could have eaten some of all of them.

We sat talking until far into the night, and she asked me how I was going to spend Christmas. I told her, "Probably in being homesick." She said that would never do and suggested that we spend it together. She said it was one of their special days and that the only happiness left her was in making some one else happy; so she had thought of cooking some nice things and going to as many sheep camps as she could, taking with her the good things to the poor exiles, the sheep-herders. I liked the plan and was glad to agree, but I never dreamed I should have so lovely a time. When the queer old wooden clock announced two we went to bed.

I left quite early the next morning with my head full of Christmas plans. You may not know, but cattle-men and sheep-men cordially hate each other. Mr. Stewart is a cattle-man, and so I didn't mention my Christmas plans to him. I saved all the butter I could spare for the sheep-herders; they never have any. That and some jars of gooseberry jelly was all I could give them. I cooked plenty for the people here, and two days before Christmas I had a chance to go down to Mrs.

Louderer's in a buggy, so we went. We found her up to her ears in cooking, and such sights and smells I could never describe. She was so glad I came early, for she needed help. I never worked so hard in my life or had a pleasanter time.

Mrs. Louderer had sent a man out several days before to find out how many camps there were and where they were located. There were twelve camps and that means twenty-four men. We roasted six geese, boiled three small hams and three hens. We had besides several meat-loaves and links of sausage. We had twelve large loaves of the *best* rye bread; a small tub of doughnuts; twelve coffee-cakes, more to be called fruit-cakes, and also a quantity of little cakes with seeds, nuts, and fruit in them,—so pretty to look at and *so* good to taste. These had a thick coat of icing, some brown, some pink, some white. I had thirteen pounds of butter and six pint jars of jelly, so we melted the jelly and poured it into twelve glasses.

The plan was, to start real early Christmas Eve morning, make our circuit of camps, and wind up the day at Frau O'Shaughnessy's to spend the night. Yes, Mrs. O'Shaughnessy is Irish,—as Irish as the pigs in Dublin. Before it was day the man came to feed and to get our horses ready. We were up betimes and had breakfast. The last speck was wiped from the shining stove, the kitchen floor was scrubbed, and the last small thing put in order. The man had four horses harnessed and hitched to the sled, on which was placed a wagon-box filled with straw, hot rocks, and blankets. Our twelve apostles—that is what we called our twelve boxes—were lifted in and tied firmly into place. Then we clambered in and away we went. Mrs. Louderer drove, and Tam O'Shanter and Paul Revere were snails compared to us.

We didn't follow any road either, but went sweeping along across country. No one else in the world could have done it unless they were drunk. We went careening along hill-sides without even slacking the trot. Occasionally we struck a particularly stubborn bunch of sagebrush and even the sled-runners would jump up into the air. We didn't stop to light, but hit the earth several feet in advance of where we left it. Luck was with us, though. I hardly expected to get through with my head unbroken, but not even a glass was cracked.

It would have done your heart good to see the sheep-men. They were all delighted, and when you consider that they live solely on canned corn and tomatoes, beans, salt pork, and coffee, you can fancy what they thought of their treat. They have mutton when it is fit to eat, but that is certainly not in winter. One man at each camp does the cooking and the other herds. It doesn't make any difference if the cook never cooked before, and most of them never did. At one camp, where we stopped for dinner, they had a most interesting collection of fossils. After delivering our last "apostle," we turned our faces toward Frau O'Shaughnessy's, and got there just in time for supper.

Mrs. O'Shaughnessy is a widow, too, and has quite an interesting story. She is a dumpy little woman whose small nose seems to be smelling the stars, it is so tip-tilted. She has the merriest blue eyes and the quickest wit. It is really worth a severe bumping just to be welcomed by her. It was so warm and cosy in her low little cabin. She had her table set for supper, but she laid plates for us and put before us a beautifully roasted chicken. Thrifty Mrs. Louderer thought it should have been saved until next day, so she said to Frau O'Shaughnessy, "We hate to eat your hen, best you save her till tomorrow." But Mrs. O'Shaughnessy answered, "Oh, 't is no mather, 't is an ould hin she was annyway." So we enjoyed the "ould hin," which was brown, juicy, and tender.

When we had finished supper and were drinking our "tay," Mrs. O'Shaughnessy told our fortunes with the tea-leaves. She told mine first and said I would die an old maid. I said it was rather late for that, but she cheerfully replied, "Oh, well, better late than niver." She predicted for Mrs. Louderer that she should shortly catch a *beau*. "'T is the next man you see that will come coortin' you." Before we left the table some one knocked and a young man, a sheep-herder, entered. He belonged to a camp a few miles away and is out from Boston in search of health. He had been into town and his horse was lamed so he could not make it into camp, and he wanted to stay overnight. He was a stranger to us all, but Mrs. O'Shaughnessy made him at home and fixed such a tempting supper for him that I am sure he was glad of the chance to stay. He was very decidedly English, and powerfully proud of it. He asked Mrs. O'Shaughnessy if she was Irish and she said, "No, ye haythen, it's Chinese Oi am. Can't yez tell it be me Cockney accint?" Mr. Boutwell looked very much surprised. I don't know which was the funnier, the way he looked or what she said.

We had a late breakfast Christmas morning, but before we were through Mr. Stewart came. We had planned to spend the day with Mrs. O'Shaughnessy, but he didn't approve of our going into the sheep district, so when he found where we had gone he came after us. Mrs. Louderer and he are old acquaintances and he bosses her around like he tries to boss me. Before we left, Mrs. O'Shaughnessy's married daughter came, so we knew she would not be lonely.

It was almost one o'clock when we got home, but all hands helped and I had plenty cooked anyway, so we soon had a good dinner on the table. Mr. Stewart had prepared a Christmas box for Jerrine and me. He doesn't approve of white waists in the winter. I had worn one at the wedding and he felt personally aggrieved. For me in the box were two dresses, that is, the material to make them. One is a brown and red checked, and the other green with a white fleck in, both outing flannel. For Jerrine there was a pair of shoes and stockings, both stockings full of candy and nuts. He is very bluff in manner, but he is really the kindest person.

Mrs. Louderer stayed until New Year's day. My Christmas was really a very happy one.

Your friend,

Elinore Rupert.

....An interesting day on this ranch is the day the cattle are named. If Mr. Stewart had children he would as soon think of leaving them unnamed as to let a "beastie" go without a name.

On the day they vaccinated he came into the kitchen and told me he would need me to help him name the "critters." So he and I "assembled" in a safe place and took turns naming the calves. As fast as a calf was vaccinated it was run out of the chute and he or I called out a name for it and it was booked that way.

The first two he named were the "Duke of Monmouth" and the "Duke of Montrose." I called my first "Oliver Cromwell" and "John Fox." The poor "mon" had to have revenge, so the next ugly, scrawny little beast he called the "Poop of Roome." And it was a heifer calf, too.

This morning I had the startling news that the "Poop" had eaten too much alfalfa and was all "swellit oop," and, moreover, he had "stealit it." I don't know which is the more astonishing, that the Pope has stolen alfalfa, or that he has eaten it.

We have a swell lot of names, but I am not sure I could tell you which is "Bloody Mary," or which is "Elizabeth," or, indeed, which is which of any of them.

E.R.

9

A Confession

Dear Mrs. Coney,—

I find upon re-reading your letter that I did not answer it at all when I wrote you. You must think me very indifferent, but I really don't mean to be.

My house joins on to Mr. Stewart's house. It was built that way so that I could "hold down" my land and job at the same time. I see the wisdom of it now, though at first I did not want it that way. My boundary lines run within two feet of Mr. Stewart's house, so it was quite easy to build on.

I think the Pattersons' ranch is about twenty-five miles from us. I am glad to tell you they are doing splendidly. Gale is just as thrifty as she can be and Bobby is steady and making money fast. Their baby is the dearest little thing. I have heard that Sedalia is to marry a Mormon bishop, but I doubt it. She puts on very disgusting airs about "our Bobby," and she patronizes Gale most shamefully; but Gale, bless her unconscious heart, is so happy in her husband and son that she doesn't know Sedalia is insulting.

My dear old grandmother whom I loved so much has gone home to God. I used to write long letters to her. I should like a few addresses of old persons who are lonely as she was, who would like letters such as I write. You know I can't be brief. I have tried and cannot. If you know of any persons who would not tire of my long accounts and would care to have them, you will be doing me a favour to let me know.

I have not treated you quite frankly about something you had a right to know about. I am ashamed and I regret very much that I have not told you. I so dread the possibility of losing your friendship that I will *never* tell you unless you promise me beforehand to forgive me. I know that is unfair, but it is the only way I can see out of a difficulty that my foolish reticence has led me into. Few people, perhaps, consider me reticent, but in some cases I am afraid I am even deceitful. Won't you make it easy to "'fess" so I may be happy again?

Truly your friend,

Elinore Rupert.

June 16, 1910.

My Dear Friend,—

Your card just to hand. I wrote you some time ago telling you I had a confession to make and have had no letter since, so thought perhaps you were scared I had done something too bad to forgive. I am suffering just now from eye-strain and can't see to write long at a time, but I reckon I had better confess and get it done with.

The thing I have done is to marry Mr. Stewart. It was such an inconsistent thing to do that I was ashamed to tell you. And, too, I was afraid you would think I didn't need your friendship and might desert me. Another of my friends thinks that way.

I hope my eyes will be better soon and then I will write you a long letter.

Your old friend with a new name,

Elinore Stewart.

10

The Story of Cora Belle

Dear Mrs. Coney,—

..... Grandma Edmonson's birthday is the 30th of May, and Mrs. O'Shaughnessy suggested that we give her a party. I had never seen Grandma, but because of something that happened in her family years ago which a few narrow-heads whom it didn't concern in the least cannot forgive or forget, I had heard much of her. The family consists of Grandma, Grandpa, and little Cora Belle, who is the sweetest little bud that ever bloomed upon the twigs of folly.

The Edmonsons had only one child, a daughter, who was to have married a man whom her parents objected to solely because he was a sheep-man, while their sympathies were with the cattle-men, although they owned only a small bunch. To gain their consent the young man closed out his interest in sheep, at a loss, filed on a splendid piece of land near them, and built a little home for the girl he loved. Before they could get to town to be married Grandpa was stricken with rheumatism. Grandma was already almost past going on with it, so they postponed the marriage, and as that winter was particularly severe, the young man took charge of the Edmonson stock and kept them from starving. As soon as he was able he went for the license.

Mrs. O'Shaughnessy and a neighbour were hunting some cattle that had wandered away and found the poor fellow shot in the back. He was not yet dead and told them it was urgently necessary for them to hurry him to the Edmonsons' and to get some one to perform the marriage ceremony as quickly as possible, for he could not live long. They told him such haste meant quicker death because he would bleed more; but he insisted, so they got a wagon and hurried all they could. But they could not outrun death. When he knew he could not

47

live to reach home, he asked them to witness all he said. Everything he possessed he left to the girl he was to have married, and said he was the father of the little child that was to come. He begged them to befriend the poor girl he had to leave in such a condition, and to take the marriage license as evidence that he had tried to do right. The wagon was stopped so the jolting would not make death any harder, and there in the shadow of the great twin buttes he died.

They took the body to the little home he had made, and Mrs. O'Shaughnessy went to the Edmonsons' to do what she could there. Poor Cora Jane didn't know how terrible a thing wounded pride is. She told her parents her misdeeds. They couldn't see that they were in any way to blame. They seemed to care nothing for her terrible sorrow nor for her weakened condition. All they could think of was that the child they had almost worshiped had disgraced them; so they told her to go.

Mrs. O'Shaughnessy took her to the home that had been prepared for her, where the poor body lay. Some way they got through those dark days, and then began the waiting for the little one to come. Poor Cora Jane said she would die then, and that she wanted to die, but she wanted the baby to know it was loved,—she wanted to leave something that should speak of that love when the child should come to understanding. So Mrs. O'Shaughnessy said they would make all its little clothes with every care, and they should tell of the love. Mrs. O'Shaughnessy is the daintiest needleworker I have ever seen; she was taught by the nuns at St. Catherine's in the "ould country." She was all patience with poor, unskilled Cora Jane, and the little outfit that was finally finished was dainty enough for a fairy. Little Cora Belle is so proud of it.

At last the time came and Mrs. O'Shaughnessy went after the parents. Long before, they had repented and were only too glad to go. The poor mother lived one day and night after the baby came. She laid the tiny thing in her mother's arms and told them to call her Cora Belle. She told them she gave them a pure little daughter in place of the sinful one they had lost.

That was almost twelve years ago, and the Edmonsons have lived in the new house all this time. The deed to the place was made out to Cora Belle, and her grandfather is her guardian. . . .

If you travelled due north from my home, after about nine hours' ride you would come into an open space in the butte lands, and away between two buttes you would see the glimmer of blue water. As you drew nearer you would be able to see the fringe of willows around the lake, and presently a low, red-roofed house with corrals and stables. You would see long lines of "buck" fence, a flock of sheep near by, and cattle scattered about feeding. This is Cora Belle's home. On the long, low porch you would see two old folks rocking. The man is small, and has rheumatism in his legs and feet so badly that he can barely hobble. The old lady is large and fat, and is also afflicted with rheumatism, but has it in her arms and shoulders. They are both cheerful and hopeful, and you would get a cordial welcome....

When you saw Cora Belle you would see a stout, square-built little figure with long flaxen braids, a pair of beautiful brown eyes and the longest and whitest lashes you ever saw, a straight nose, a short upper lip, a broad, full forehead,—the whole face, neither pretty nor ugly, plentifully sown with the brownest freckles. She is very truly the head of the family, doing all the housework and looking after the stock, winter and summer, entirely by herself. Three years ago she took things into her own hands, and since that time has managed altogether. Mrs. O'Shaughnessy, however, tells her what to do.

The sheep, forty in number, are the result of her individual efforts. Mrs. O'Shaughnessy told her there was more money in raising lambs than in raising chickens, so she quit the chickens as a business and went to some of the big sheep-men and got permission to take the "dogie" lambs, which they are glad to give away. She had plenty of cows, so she milked cows and fed lambs all day long all last year. This year she has forty head of nice sheep worth four dollars each, and she doesn't have to feed them the year round as she would chickens, and the wolves are no worse to kill sheep than they are to kill chickens.

When shearing-time came she went to a sheep-man and told him she would help cook for his men one week if he would have her sheep sheared with his. She said her work was worth three dollars, that is what one man would get a day shearing, and he could easily shear her sheep in one day. That is how she got her sheep sheared. The man had her wool hauled to town with his, sold it for her, and it brought sixty dollars. She took her money to Mrs. O'Shaughnessy. She wanted some supplies ordered before she went home, because, as she gravely said, "the rheumatiz would get all the money she had left when she got home,"—meaning that her grandparents would spend what remained for medicine.

The poor old grandparents read all the time of wonderful cures that different dopes accomplish, and they spend every nickel they can get their hands on for nostrums. They try everything they read of, and have to buy it by the case,—horrid patent stuff! They have rolls of testimonials and believe every word, so they keep on trying and hoping. When there is any money they each order whatever medicine they want to try. If Mrs. Edmonson's doesn't seem to help her, Grandpa takes it and she takes his,—that is their idea of economy. They would spend hours telling you about their different remedies and would offer you spoonful after spoonful of vile-looking liquid, and be mildly grieved when you refused to take it. Grandma's hands are so bent and twisted that she can't sew, so dear old Grandpa tries to do it.

Mrs. O'Shaughnessy told me that she helped out when she could. Three years ago she made them all a complete outfit, but the "rheumatiz" has been getting all the spare money since then, so there has been nothing to sew. A peddler sold them a piece of gingham which they made up for Cora Belle. It was broad pink and white stripes, and they wanted some style to "Cory's" clothes, so they cut a gored skirt. But they had no pattern and made the gores by folding a width of the goods biasly and cutting it that way. It was put together with no regard to matching the stripes, and a bias seam came in the centre behind, but they put no stay in the seam and the result was the most outrageous affair imaginable.

Well, we had a large room almost empty and Mr. Stewart liked the idea of a party, so Mrs. Louderer, Mrs. O'Shaughnessy, and myself planned for the event. It was to be a sewing-bee, a few good neighbours invited, and all to sew for Grandma.... So Mrs. O'Shaughnessy went to Grandma's and got all the material she had to make up. I had saved some sugar-bags and some flour-bags. I knew Cora Belle needed underwear, so I made her some little petticoats of the larger bags and some drawers of the smaller. I had a small piece of white lawn that I had no use for, and of that I made a dear little sunbonnet with a narrow edging of lace around, and also made a gingham bonnet for her. Two days before the time, came Mrs. Louderer, laden with bundles, and Mrs. O'Shaughnessy, also laden.

We had all been thinking of Cora Belle. Mr. Stewart had sent by mail for her a pair of sandals for everyday wear and a nice pair of shoes, also some stockings. Mrs. Louderer brought cloth for three dresses of heavy Dutch calico, and gingham for three aprons. She made them herself and she sews so carefully. She had bought patterns and the little dresses were stylishly made, as well as well made. Mrs. O'Shaughnessy brought a piece of crossbar with a tiny forget-me-not polka dot, and also had goods and embroidery for a suit of underwear. My own poor efforts were already completed when the rest came, so I was free to help them.

Late in the afternoon of the 29th a funny something showed up. Fancy a squeaky, rickety old wagon without a vestige of paint. The tires had come off and had been "set" at home; that is done by heating the tires red-hot and having the rims of the wheels covered with several layers of burlap, or other old rags, well wet; then the red-hot tire is put on and water hurriedly poured on to shrink the iron and to keep the burlap from blazing. Well, whoever had set Cora Belle's tyres had forgotten to cut away the surplus burlap, so all the ragtags were merrily waving in the breeze.

Cora Belle's team would bring a smile to the soberest face alive. Sheba is a tall, lanky old mare. Once she was bay in colour, but the years have added gray hair until now she is roan. Being so long-legged she strides along at an amazing pace which her mate, Balaam, a little donkey, finds it hard to keep up with. Balaam, like Sheba, is full of years. Once his glossy brown coat was the pride of some Mexican's heart, but time has added to his colour also, and now he is blue. His eyes are sunken and dim, his ears no longer stand up in true donkey style, but droop dejectedly. He has to trot his best to keep up with Sheba's slowest stride. About every three miles he balks, but little Cora Belle doesn't call it balking, she says Balaam has stopped to rest, and they sit and wait till he is ready to trot along again. That is the kind of layout which drew up before our door that evening.

Cora Belle was driving and she wore her wonderful pink dress which hung down in a peak behind, fully six inches longer than anywhere else. The poor child had no shoes. The winter had tried the last pair to their utmost endurance and the "rheumatiz" had long since got the last dollar, so she came with her chubby little sunburned legs bare. Her poor little scarred feet were clean, her toe-nails full of nicks almost into the quick, broken against rocks when she had been herding her sheep. In the back of the wagon, flat on the bottom, sat Grandma and Grandpa, such bundles of coats and blankets I can't describe. After a great deal of trouble we got them unloaded and into the house. Then Mrs. Louderer entertained them while Mrs. O'Shaughnessy and I prepared supper and got a bath ready for Cora Belle. We had a T-bone steak, mashed potatoes, hominy, hot biscuits and butter, and stewed prunes. Their long ride had made them hungry and I know they enjoyed their meal.

After supper Cora Belle and I washed the dishes while Mrs. O'Shaughnessy laid out the little clothes. Cora Belle's clothes were to be a surprise. The postmistress here also keeps a small store and has ribbon, and when she heard of our plans from Mr. Stewart she sent up a couple of pairs of hair-ribbon for Cora Belle. Soon Mrs. O'Shaughnessy called us, and Cora Belle and I went into the bedroom where she was. I wish you could have seen that child! Poor little neglected thing, she began to cry. She said, "They ain't for me, I know they ain't. Why, it ain't my birthday, it's Granny's." Nevertheless, she had her arms full of them and was clutching them so tightly with her work-worn little hands that we couldn't get them. She sobbed so deeply that Grandma heard her and became alarmed. She hobbled to the door and pounded with her poor twisted hands, calling all the while, "Cory, Cory Belle, what ails you?" She got so excited that I opened the door, but Cora Belle told her to go away. She said, "They ain't for you, Granny, and they ain't for me either." . . .

People here observe Decoration Day faithfully, and Cora Belle had brought half a wagon-load of iris, which grows wild here. Next morning we were all up early, but Cora Belle's flowers had wilted and she had to gather more, but we all hurried and helped. She said as she was going to see her mother she wanted to wear her prettiest dress, so Gale and Mrs. O'Shaughnessy helped her to get ready. The cemetery is only about two miles away, so we were all down quite early. We were obliged to hurry because others were coming to help sew. Cora Belle went at once to the graves where her parents lie side by side, and began talking to her mother just as though she saw her. "You didn't know me, did you, Mother, with my pretty new things? But I am your little girl, Mamma. I am your little Cora Belle."

After she had talked and had turned every way like a proud little bird, she went to work. And, oh, how fast she worked! Both graves were first completely covered with pine boughs. It looked like sod, so closely were the little twigs laid. Next she broke the stems off the iris and scattered the blossoms over, and the effect was very beautiful. Then we hurried home and everybody got busy. The men took Grandpa off to another part of the ranch where they were fanning oats to plant, and kept him all day. That was good for him because then he could be with the men all day and he so seldom has a chance to be with men. Several ladies came and they all made themselves at home and worked like beavers, and we all had a fine time....

Sedalia was present and almost caused a riot. She says she likes unusual words because they lend distinction to conversation. Well, they do—sometimes. There was another lady present whose children are very gifted musically, but who have the bad name of taking what they want without asking. The mother can neither read nor write, and she is very sensitive about the bad name her children have. While we were all busy some one made a remark about how smart these children were. Sedalia thought that a good time to get in a big word, so she said, "Yes, I have always said Lula was a progeny." Mrs. Hall didn't know what she meant and thought that she was casting reflections on her child's honesty, so with her face scarlet and her eyes blazing she said, "Sedalia Lane, I won't allow you nor nobody else to say my child is a progeny. You can take that back or I will slap you peaked." Sedalia took it back in a hurry, so I guess little Lula Hall is not a progeny.

Everyone left about four except Gale, Mrs. O'Shaughnessy, Mrs. Louderer, and the Edmonsons. They had farthest to go, so they stayed over night again. We worked until ten o'clock that night over Grandma's clothes, but everything was thoroughly finished. Every button was on, every thread-end knotted and clipped, and some tired workers lay down to rest, as did a very happy child and a very thankful old lady.

Everyone got away by ten o'clock the next morning. The last I saw of little Cora Belle was when they had reached the top of a long slope and Balaam had "stopped to rest." The breeze from the south was playfully fluttering the rags on the wheels. Presently I heard a long "hee-haw, hee-haw," and I knew Balaam had rested and had started.

I have been a very busy woman since I began this letter to you several days ago. A dear little child has joined the angels. I dressed him and helped to make his casket. There is no minister in this whole country and I could not bear the little broken lily-bud to be just carted away and buried, so I arranged the funeral and conducted the services. I know I am unworthy and in no way fitted for such a mission, but I did my poor best, and if no one else is comforted, I am. I know the message of God's love and care has been told once, anyway, to people who have learned to believe more strongly in hell than in heaven.

Dear friend, I do hope that this New Year will bring you and yours fuller joys than you have ever known. If I had all the good gifts in my hands you should certainly be blessed.

Your sincere friend,

Elinore Rupert Stewart.

11

Zebbie's Story

September 1, 1910.

Dear Mrs. Coney,—

It was just a few days after the birthday party and Mrs. O'Shaughnessy was with me again. We were down at the barn looking at some new pigs, when we heard the big corral gates swing shut, so we hastened out to see who it could be so late in the day.

It was Zebbie. He had come on the stage to Burnt Fork and the driver had brought him on here.... There was so much to tell, and he whispered he had something to tell me privately, but that he was too tired then; so after supper I hustled him off to bed....

Next morning ... the men went off to their work and Zebbie and I were left to tell secrets. When he was sure we were alone he took from his trunk a long, flat box. Inside was the most wonderful shirt I have ever seen; it looked like a cross between a nightshirt and a shirt-waist. It was of homespun linen. The bosom was ruffled and tucked, all done by hand,—such tiny stitches, such patience and skill. Then he handed me an old daguerreotype. I unfastened the little golden hook and inside was a face good to see and to remember. It was dim, yet clear in outline, just as if she were looking out from the mellow twilight of long ago. The sweet, elusive smile,—I couldn't tell where it was, whether it was the mouth or the beautiful eyes that were smiling. All that was visible of her dress was the Dutch collar, just like what is being worn now. It was pinned with an ugly old brooch which Zebbie said was a "breast-pin" he had given her. Under the glass on the other side was a strand of faded hair and a slip of paper. The writing on the paper was so faded it was scarcely readable, but it said: "Pauline Gorley, age 22, 1860."

Next he showed me a note written by Pauline, simply worded, but it held a world of meaning for Zebbie. It said:

"I spun and wove this cloth at Adeline's, enough for me a dress and you a shirt, which I made. It is for the wedding, else to be buried in. Yours, Pauline."

The shirt, the picture, and the note had waited for him all these years in Mothie's care. And now I will tell you the story.

Long, long ago someone did something to someone else and started a feud. Unfortunately the Gorleys were on one side and the Parkers on the other. That it all happened before either Zebbie or Pauline was born made no difference. A Gorley must hate a Parker always, as also a Parker must hate a Gorley. Pauline was the only girl, and she had a regiment of big brothers who gloried in the warfare and wanted only the slightest pretext to shoot a Parker. So they grew up, and Zebbie often met Pauline at the quiltings and other gatherings at the homes of non-partisans. He remembers her so perfectly and describes her so plainly that I can picture her easily. She had brown eyes and hair. She used to ride about on her sorrel palfrey with her "nigger" boy Cæsar on behind to open and shut plantation gates. She wore a pink calico sunbonnet, and Zebbie says "she was just like the pink hollyhocks that grew by mother's window." Isn't that a sweet picture?

Her mother and father were both dead, and she and her brothers lived on their plantation. Zebbie had never dared speak to her until one day he had driven over with his mother and sisters to a dinner given on a neighbouring plantation. He was standing outside near the wall, when some one dropped a spray of apple blossoms down upon him from an upper window. He looked up and Pauline was leaning out smiling at him. After that he made it a point to frequent places where he might expect her, and things went so well that presently Cæsar was left at home lest he should tell the brothers. She was a loyal little soul and would not desert, although he urged her to, even promising to go away, "plumb away, clean to Scott County if she would go." She told him that her brothers would go even as far as that to kill him, so that they must wait and hope. Finally Zebbie got tired of waiting, and one day he boldly rode up to the Gorley home and formally asked for Pauline's hand. The bullet he got for his presumption kept him from going to the war with his father and brother when they marched away.

Sometime later George Gorley was shot and killed from ambush, and although Zebbie had not yet left his bed the Gorleys believed he did it, and one night Pauline came through a heavy rainstorm, with only Cæsar, to warn Zebbie and to beg him, for her sake, to get away as fast as he could that night. She pleaded that she could not live if he were killed and could never marry him if he killed her brothers, so she persuaded him to go while they were all innocent.

Well, he did as she wished and they never saw each other again. He never went home again until last Thanksgiving, and dear little Pauline had been dead for years. She herself had taken her little gifts for Zebbie to Mothie to keep for him. Some years later she died and was buried in the dress she mentioned. It was woven at Adeline Carter's, one of the bitterest enemies of the Gorleys, but the sacrifice of her pride did her no good because she was long at rest before Zebbie knew. He had been greatly grieved because no stone marked her grave, only a tangle of rose-briers. So he bought a stone, and in the night before Decoration Day he and two of Uncle Buck's grandsons went to the Gorley burying-ground and raised it to the memory of sweet Pauline. Some of the Gorleys still live there, so he came home at once, fearing if they should find out who placed the stone above their sister they would take vengeance on his poor, frail body.

After he had finished telling me his story, I felt just as I used to when Grandmother opened the "big chist" to air her wedding clothes and the dress each of her babies wore when baptized. It seemed almost like smelling the lavender and rose-leaves, and it was with reverent fingers that I folded the shirt, the work of love, yellow with age, and laid it in the box....

Well, Mrs. O'Shaughnessy returned, and early one morning we started with a wagon and a bulging mess-box for Zebbie's home. We were going a new and longer route in order to take the wagon. Dandelions spread a carpet of gold. Larkspur grew waist-high with its long spikes of blue. The service-bushes and the wild cherries were a mass of white beauty. Meadowlarks and robins and bluebirds twittered and sang from every branch, it almost seemed. A sky of tenderest blue bent over us and fleecy little clouds drifted lazily across. . . . Soon we came to the pineries, where we travelled up deep gorges and *cañons*. The sun shot arrows of gold through the pines down upon us and we gathered our arms full of columbines. The little black squirrels barked and chattered saucily as we passed along, and we were all children together. We forgot all about feuds and partings, death and hard times. All we remembered was that God is good and the world is wide and beautiful. We plodded along all day. Next morning there was a blue haze that Zebbie said meant there would be a high wind, so we hurried to reach his home that evening.

The sun was hanging like a great red ball in the smoky haze when we entered the long *cañon* in which is Zebbie's cabin. Already it was dusky in the *cañons* below, but not a breath of air stirred. A more delighted man than Zebbie I never saw when we finally drove up to his low, comfortable cabin. Smoke was slowly rising from the chimney, and Gavotte, the man in charge, rushed out and the hounds set up a joyful barking. Gavotte is a Frenchman, and he was all smiles and gesticulations as he said, "Welcome, welcome! Today I am rejoice you have come. Yesterday I am despair if you have come because I am scrub, but today, behold, I am delight."

I have heard of clean people, but Gavotte is the cleanest man I ever saw. The cabin floor was so white I hated to step upon it. The windows shone, and at each there was a calico curtain, blue-and-white check, unironed but newly washed. In one window was an old brown pitcher, cracked and nicked, filled with thistles. I never thought them pretty before, but the pearly pink and the silvery green were so pretty and looked so clean that they had a new beauty. Above the fireplace was a great black eagle which Gavotte had killed, the wings outspread and a bunch of arrows in the claws. In one corner near the fire was a washstand, and behind it hung the fishing-tackle. Above one door was a gun-rack, on which lay the rifle and shotgun, and over the other door was a pair of deer-antlers. In the centre of the room stood the square home-made table, every inch scrubbed. In the side room, which is the bedroom, was a wide bunk made of pine plank that had also been scrubbed, then filled with fresh, sweet pine boughs, and over them was spread a piece of canvas that had once been a wagon sheet, but Gavotte had washed it and boiled and pounded it until it was clean and sweet. That served for a sheet.

Zebbie was beside himself with joy. The hounds sprang upon him and expressed their joy unmistakably. He went at once to the corrals to see the "critters," and every one of them was safely penned for the night. "Old Sime," an old ram (goodness knows *how* old!), promptly butted him over, but he just beamed with pleasure. "Sime knows me, dinged if he don't!" was his happy exclamation. We went into the cabin and left him fondling the "critters."

Gavotte did himself proud getting supper. We had trout and the most delicious biscuit. Each of us had a crisp, tender head of lettuce with a spoonful of potato salad in the center. We had preserves made from canned peaches, and the firmest yellow butter. Soon it was quite

57

dark and we had a tiny brass lamp which gave but a feeble light, but it was quite cool so we had a blazing fire which made it light enough.

When supper was over, Zebbie called us out and asked us if we could hear anything. We could hear the most peculiar, long-drawn, sighing wail that steadily grew louder and nearer. I was really frightened, but he said it was the forerunner of the windstorm that would soon strike us. He said it was wind coming down Crag Cañon, and in just a few minutes it struck us like a cold wave and rushed, sighing, on down the *cañon*. We could hear it after it had passed us, and it was perfectly still around the cabin. Soon we heard the deep roaring of the coming storm, and Zebbie called the hounds in and secured the door. The sparks began to fly up the chimney. Jerrine lay on a bearskin before the fire, and Mrs. O'Shaughnessy and I sat on the old blue "settle" at one side. Gavotte lay on the other side of the fire on the floor, his hands under his head. Zebbie got out his beloved old fiddle, tuned up, and began playing.

Outside the storm was raging, growing worse all the time. Zebbie played and played. The worse the tumult, the harder the storm, the harder he played. I remember I was holding my breath, expecting the house to be blown away every moment, and Zebbie was playing what he called "Bonaparte's Retreat." It all seemed to flash before me—I could see those poor, suffering soldiers staggering along in the snow, sacrifices to one man's unholy ambition. I verily believe we were all bewitched. I shouldn't have been surprised to have seen witches and gnomes come tumbling down the chimney or flying in at the door, riding on the crest of the storm. I glanced at Mrs. O'Shaughnessy. She sat with her chin in her hand, gazing with unseeing eyes into the fire. Zebbie seemed possessed; he couldn't tire.

It seemed like hours had passed and the tumult had not diminished. I felt like shrieking, but I gathered Jerrine up into my arms and carried her in to bed. Mrs. O'Shaughnessy came with us. She touched my elbow and said, "Child, don't look toward the window, the banshees are out tonight." We knelt together beside the bed and said our beads; then, without undressing save pulling off our shoes, we crawled under our blankets and lay on the sweet, clean pine. We were both perfectly worn out, but we could not sleep. There seemed to be hundreds of different noises of the storm, for there are so many *cañons*, so many crooks and turns, and the great forest too. The wind was shrieking, howling, and roaring all at once. A deep boom announced the fall of some giant of the forest. I finally dozed off even in that terrible din,

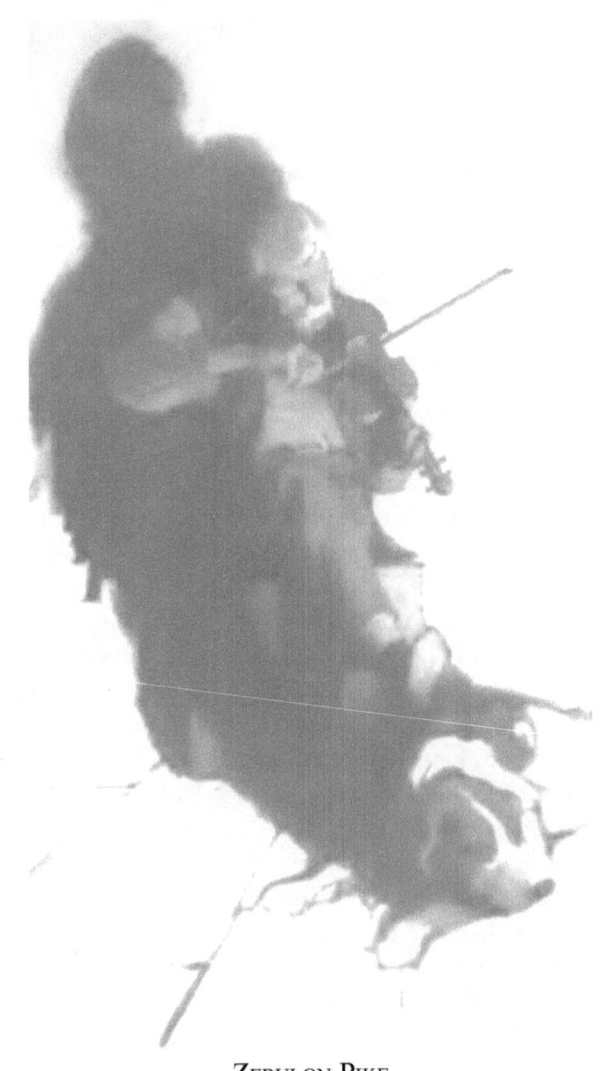

ZEBULON PIKE

but Zebbie was not so frenzied as he had been. He was playing "Annie Laurie," and that song has always been a favourite of mine. The storm began gradually to die away and "Annie Laurie" sounded so beautiful. I was thinking of Pauline and, I know, to Zebbie, Annie Laurie and Pauline Gorley are one and the same.

I knew no more until I heard Zebbie call out, "Ho, you sleepy-heads, it's day." Mrs. O'Shaughnessy turned over and said she was still sleepy. My former visit had taught me what beauty the early morning would spread before me, so I dressed hastily and went outdoors. Zebbie called me to go for a little walk. The amber light of the new day was chasing the violet and amethyst shadows down the *cañons*. It was all more beautiful than I can tell you. On one side the *cañon*-walls were almost straight up. It looked as if we might step off into a very world of mountains. Soon Old Baldy wore a crown of gleaming gold. The sun was up. We walked on and soon came to a brook. We were washing our faces in its icy waters when we heard twigs breaking, so we stood perfectly still. From out the undergrowth of birch and willows came a deer with two fawns. They stopped to drink, and nibbled the bushes. But soon they scented strangers, and, looking about with their beautiful, startled eyes, they saw us and away they went like the wind. We saw many great trees uptorn by the storm. High up on the cliffs Zebbie showed me where the eagles built every year. . . .

We turned homeward and sat down upon the trunk of a fallen pine to rest and take another look at the magnificent view. Zebbie was silent, but presently he threw a handful of pebbles down the *cañon* wall. "I am not sorry Pauline is dead. I have never shed a tear. I know you think that is odd, but I have never wanted to mourn. I am glad that it is as it is. I am happy and at peace because I know she is mine. The little breeze is Pauline's own voice; she had a little caressing way just like the gentlest breeze when it stirs your hair. There is something in everything that brings back Pauline: the beauty of the morning, the song of a bird or the flash of its wings. The flowers look like she did. So I have not lost her, she is mine more than ever. I have always felt so, but was never quite sure until I went back and saw where they laid her. I know people think I am crazy, but I don't care for that. I shall not hate to die. When you get to be as old as I am, child, everything will have a new meaning to you."

At last we slowly walked back to the cabin, and at breakfast Zebbie told of the damage the storm had done. He was so common-place that no one ever would have guessed his strange fancy. . . .

I shall never forget Zebbie as I last saw him. It was the morning we started home. After we left the bench that Zebbie lives on, our road wound down into a deeper *cañon*. Zebbie had followed us to where a turn in the *cañon* should hide us from view. I looked back and saw him standing on the cliffs, high above us, the early morning sun turning his snowy hair to gold, the breeze-fingers of Pauline tossing the scanty locks. I shall always remember him so, a living monument to a dead past.

Elinore Stewart.

12

A Contented Couple

Dear Mrs. Coney,—

.... I once "heared" Sedalia Lane telling some of her experiences, and she said she "surreptitiously stole along." One day, when I thought the coast was clear, I was surreptitiously examining the contents of the tool-chest with a view toward securing to myself such hammers, saws, and what else I might need in doing some carpentry work I had planned. The tool-chest is kept in the granary; both it and the granary are usually kept locked. Now the "gude mon" has an idea that a "wooman" needs no tools, and the use and misuse of his tools have led to numbers of inter-household wars. I was gloating over my opportunity, and also making the best of it, when a medley of burring Scotch voices brought me to a quick realisation that discretion is the better part of valour. So I went into seclusion behind a tall oat-bin.

It seemed that two neighbours whom I had never seen were preparing to go to town, and had come to get some tools and to see if the Stewart would lend them each a team. Now Mr. Stewart must be very righteous, because he certainly regardeth his beast, although he doesn't always love his neighbour as himself. He was willing, however, for friends Tam Campbell and Archie McEttrick to use his teams, but he himself would take a lighter rig and go along, so as to see that his horses were properly cared for, and to help out in case of need.

They made their plans, set the day, and went their ways. As soon as I could, I made myself scarce about the granary and very busy about the house, and, like Josiah Allen, I was in a very "happyfied" state of mind. There is nothing Mr. Stewart likes better than to catch me unprepared for something. I had been wanting to go to town, and he had said I might go with him next time he went, if I was ready when he was. I knew I would not hear one word about the proposed trip, but that only added to the fun. I had plenty of time to make all preparations; so the day before they were to start found me with all in readiness. It was quite early in the spring and the evenings were quite chilly. We had just finished supper, when we heard a great rumbling, and I knew neighbours Campbell and McEttrick had arrived on their way to town; so I began to prepare supper for them. I hadn't expected a woman, and was surprised when I saw the largest, most ungainly person I have ever met come shambling toward me.

She was Aggie McEttrick. She is tall and raw-boned, she walks with her toes turned out, she has a most peculiar lurching gait like a camel's. She has skin the colour of a new saddle, and the oddest straggly straw-coloured hair. She never wears corsets and never makes her waists long enough, so there is always a streak of gray undershirt visible about her waist. Her skirts are never long enough either, and she knits her own stockings. Those inclined can always get a good glimpse of blue-and-white striped hose. She said, "I guess you are the Missus." And that was every word she said until I had supper on the table. The men were busy with their teams, and she sat with her feet in my oven, eyeing my every movement.

I told her we had just had our supper, but she waited until I had theirs ready before she announced that neither she nor Archie ate hot biscuits or steak, that they didn't take tea for supper, preferred coffee, and that neither of them could eat peaches or honey. So all of my supper was ruled off except the butter and cream. She went down to their wagons and brought up what she wanted, so Tam Campbell was the only one who ate my honey and biscuit.

Tam is just a Scot with an amazingly close fist, and he is very absent-minded. I had met Annie, his wife, and their six children. She told me of his absent-mindedness. Her remedy for his trouble when it came to household needs was to repeat the article two or three times in the list. People out like we are buy a year's supply at a time. So a list of needed things is made up and sent into town. Tam always managed to forget a great many things.

Well, bedtime came. I offered to show them to their room, but Aggie said, "We'll nae sleep in your bed. We'll jest bide in the kitchen." I could not persuade her to change her mind. Tam slept at the barn in order to see after the "beasties," should they need attention during the night. As I was preparing for bed, Aggie thrust her head into my room and announced that she would be up at three o'clock. I am not an early bird, so I thought I would let Aggie get her own breakfast, and I told her she would find everything in the pantry. As long as I was awake I could hear Archie and Aggie talking, but I could not imagine what about. I didn't know their habits so well as I came to later. Next morning the rumbling of their wagons awakened me, but I turned over and slept until after six.

There are always so many things to do before leaving that it was nine o'clock before we got started. We had only gotten about two miles, when Mr. Stewart remembered he had not locked the granary, so back we trotted. We nooned only a few miles from home. We knew we could not catch the wagons before camping-time unless we drove very hard, so Mr. Stewart said we would go by the Edmonsons' and spend the night there. I enjoy even the memory of that drive through the short spring afternoon,—the warm red sand of the desert; the Wind River Mountains wrapped in the blue veil of distance; the sparse gray-green sage, ugly in itself, but making complete a beautiful picture; the occasional glimpse we had of shy, beautiful wild creatures. So much happiness can be crowded into so short a time. I was glad, though, when Cora Belle's home became a part of our beautiful picture. It is situated among great red buttes, and there is a blue lake back of the house. Around the lake is a fringe of willows. Their house is a low, rambling affair, with a long, low porch and a red clay roof. Before the house is a cotton-wood tree, its gnarled, storm-twisted branches making it seem to have the "rheumatiz." There is a hop-vine at one end of the porch. It had not come out when we were there, but the dead vine clung hopelessly to its supports.

Little Cora Belle just bubbled with delight, and her grandparents were scarcely better than she. Spring house-cleaning was just finished, and they have company so seldom that they made us feel that we were doing them a favour by stopping. Poor old "Pa" hobbled out to help put the team away, and when they came back, Cora Belle asked me out to help prepare supper, so I left Mr. Stewart with "Granny" and "Pa" to listen to their recitals and to taste their many medicines. Cora Belle is really an excellent housekeeper. Her cooking would surprise many people. Her bread was delicious, and I am sure I never tasted anything better than the roasted leg of lamb she gave us for supper. I am ashamed to tell you how much I ate of her carrot jam. From where I sat I had a splendid view of the sunset across the lake. Speaking of things singly, Wyoming has nothing beautiful to offer. Taken altogether, it is grandly beautiful, and at sunrise and sunset the "heavens declare His glory."

Cora Belle is so animated and so straightforward, so entirely clean in all her thoughts and actions, that she commands love and respect at one and the same time. After supper her grandfather asked her to sing and play for us. Goodness only knows where they got the funny little old organ that Cora Belle thinks so much of. It has spots all over it of medicine that has been spilled at different times, and it has, as Cora Belle said, lost its voice in spots; but that doesn't set back Cora Belle at all, she plays away just as if it was all right. Some of the keys keep up a mournful whining and groaning, entirely outside of the tune. Cora Belle says they play themselves. After several "pieces" had been endured, "Pa" said, "Play my piece, Cory Belle"; so we had "Bingen on the Rhine" played and sung from A to izzard.

Dear old "Pa," his pain-twisted old face just beamed with pride. I doubt if heaven will have for him any sweeter music than his "baby's" voice. Granny's squeaky, trembly old voice trailed in after Cora Belle's, always a word or two behind. "Tell my friends and companions when they meet and *scrouge* around"; that is the way they sang it, but no one would have cared for that, if they had noticed with what happy eagerness the two sang together. The grandparents would like to have sat up all night singing and telling of things that happened in bygone days, but poor tired little Cora Belle began to nod, so we retired. As we were preparing for bed it suddenly occurred to Mr. Stewart that I had not been surprised when going to town was mentioned, so he said, "Wooman, how did it happen that you were ready when I was to gae to the toone?"

"Oh," I said, "I knew you were going."

"Who tell it ye?"

"A little bird."

"'T was some fool wooman, mayhap."

I didn't feel it necessary to enlighten him, and I think he is still wondering how I knew.

Next morning we were off early, but we didn't come up with the wagons until almost camping-time. The great heavily-loaded wagons were creaking along over the heavy sands. The McEttricks were behind, Aggie's big frame swaying and lurching with every jolt of the wagon. They never travel without their German socks. They are great thick things to wear on the outside of their shoes. As we came up behind them, we could see Aggie's big socks dangling and bobbing beside Archie's from where they were tied on the back part of the wagon. We could hear them talking and see them gesticulating. When we came nearer, we found they were quarrelling, and they kept at it as long as I was awake that night. After the men had disposed of their loads, they and Mr. Stewart were going out of town to where a new coal-mine was being opened. I intended to go on the train to Rock Springs to do some shopping. Aggie said she was going also. I suggested that we get a room together, as we would have to wait several hours for the train, but she was suspicious of my motives. She is greatly afraid of being "done," so she told me to get my own room and pay for it. We got into town about three o'clock in the afternoon, and the train left at midnight.

I had gone to my room, and Jerrine and myself were enjoying a good rest after our fatiguing drive, when my door was thrown open and a very angry Aggie strode in. They asked us fifty cents each for our rooms. Aggie paid hers under protest and afterward got to wondering how long she was entitled to its use. She had gone back to the clerk about it, and he had told her for that night only. She argued that she should have her room for a quarter, as she would only use it until midnight. When that failed, she asked for her money back, but the clerk was out of patience and refused her that. Aggie was angry all through. She vowed she was being robbed. After she had berated me soundly for submitting so tamely, she flounced back to her own room, declaring she would get even with the robbers.

I had to hurry like everything that night to get myself and Jerrine ready for the train, so I could spare no time for Aggie. She was not at the depot, and Jerrine and I had to go on to Rock Springs without her. It is only a couple of hours from Green River to Rock Springs, so I had a good nap and a late breakfast. I did my shopping and was back at Green River at two that afternoon. The first person I saw was Aggie. She sat in the depot, glowering at everybody. She had a basket of eggs and a pail of butter, which she had been trying to sell. She was waiting for the night train, the only one she could get to Rock Springs. I asked her had she overslept. "No, I didna," she replied. Then, she proceeded to tell me that, as she had paid for a whole night's use of a room, she had stayed to get its use. That it had made her plans miscarry didn't seem to count.

After all our business was attended to, we started for home. The wagons were half a day ahead of us. When we came in sight, we could see Aggie fanning the air with her long arms, and we knew they were quarrelling. I remarked that I could not understand how persons who hated each other so could live together. Clyde told me I had much to learn, and said that really he knew of no other couple who were actually so devoted. He said to prove it I should ask Aggie into the buggy with me and he would get in with Archie, and afterwards we would compare notes. He drove up alongside of them, and Aggie seemed glad to make the exchange. As we had the buggy, we drove ahead of the wagons. It seems that Archie and Aggie are each jealous of the other. Archie is as ugly a little monkey as it would be possible to imagine. She bemeaned him until at last I asked her why she didn't leave him, and added that I would not stand such crankiness for one moment. Then she poured out the vials of her wrath upon my head, only I don't think they were vials but barrels.

About sundown we made it to where we intended to camp and found that Mrs. O'Shaughnessy had established a sheep-camp there, and was out with her herd herself, having only Manny, a Mexican boy she had brought up herself, for a herder. She welcomed us cordially and began supper for our entire bunch. Soon the wagons came, and all was confusion for a few minutes getting the horses put away for the night. Aggie went to her wagon as soon as it stopped and made secure her butter and eggs against a possible raid by Mrs. O'Shaughnessy. Having asked too high a price for them, she had failed to sell them and was taking them back.

After supper we were sitting around the fire, Tam going over his account and lamenting that because of his absent-mindedness he had bought a whole hundred pounds of sugar more than he had intended, Aggie and Archie silent for once, pouting I suspect. Clyde smiled across the camp-fire at me and said, "Gin ye had sic a lass as I hae, ye might blither."

"Gin ye had sic a mon as mine—" I began, but Mrs. O'Shaughnessy said, "Gin ye had sic a mon as I hae."

Then we all three laughed, for we had each heard the same thing, and we knew the McEttricks wouldn't fight each other. They suspected us of laughing at them, for Archie said to Aggie, "Aggie, lass, is it sport they are making of our love?"

"'T is daft they be, Archie, lad; we'll nae mind their blither." She arose and shambled across to Archie and hunkered her big self down beside him. We went to bed and left them peaceable for once.

I am really ashamed of the way I have treated you, but I know you will forgive me. I am not strong yet, and my eyes are still bothering me, but I hope to be all right soon now, and I promise you a better letter next time. Jerrine is very proud of her necklace. I think they are so nice for children. I can remember how proud I was of mine when I was a child. Please give your brother our thanks, and tell him his little gift made my little girl very happy.

I am afraid this letter will seem rather jumbled. I still want the address of your friend in Salem or any other. I shall find time to write, and I am not going to let my baby prevent me from having many enjoyable outings. We call our boy Henry Clyde for his father. He is a dear little thing, but he is a lusty yeller for baby's rights.

With much love,

Jerrine and her Mamma.

13

Proving Up

Dear Mrs. Coney,—

I think you must be expecting an answer to your letter by now, so I will try to answer as many of your questions as I remember. Your letter has been mislaid. We have been very much rushed all this week. We had the thresher crew two days. I was busy cooking for them two days before they came, and have been busy ever since cleaning up after them. Clyde has taken the thresher on up the valley to thresh for the neighbours, and all the men have gone along, so the children and I are alone. No, I shall not lose my land, although it will be over two years before I can get a deed to it. The five years in which I am required to "prove up" will have passed by then. I couldn't have held my homestead if Clyde had also been proving up, but he had accomplished that years ago and has his deed, so I am allowed my homestead.

Also I have not yet used my desert right, so I am still entitled to one hundred and sixty acres more. I shall file on that much some day when I have sufficient money of my own earning. The law requires a cash payment of twenty-five cents per acre at the filing, and one dollar more per acre when final proof is made. I should not have married if Clyde had not promised I should meet all my land difficulties unaided. I wanted the fun and the experience. For that reason I want to earn every cent that goes into my own land and improvements myself. Sometimes I almost have a brain-storm wondering how I am going to do it, but I know I shall succeed; other women have succeeded. I know of several who are now where they can laugh at past trials. Do you know?—I am a firm believer in laughter. I am real superstitious about it. I think if Bad Luck came along, he would take to his heels if some one laughed right loudly.

I think Jerrine must be born for the law. She always threshes out questions that arise, to her own satisfaction, if to no one else's. She prayed for a long time for her brother; also she prayed for some puppies. The puppies came, but we didn't let her know they were here until they were able to walk. One morning she saw them following their mother, so she danced for joy. When her little brother came she was plainly disappointed. "Mamma," she said, "did God really make the baby?"

"Yes, dear."

"Then He hasn't treated us fairly, and I should like to know why. The puppies could walk when He finished them; the calves can, too. The pigs can, and the colt, and even the chickens. What is the use of giving us a half-finished baby? He has no hair, and no teeth; he can't walk or talk, nor do anything else but squall and sleep."

After many days she got the question settled. She began right where she left off. "I know, Mamma, why God gave us such a half-finished baby; so he could learn our ways, and no one else's, since he must live with us, and so we could learn to love him. Every time I stand beside his buggy he laughs and then I love him, but I don't love Stella nor Marvin because they laugh. So that is why." Perhaps that is the reason.

Zebbie's kinsfolk have come and taken him back to Yell County. I should not be surprised if he never returned. The Lanes and the Pattersons leave shortly for Idaho, where "our Bobbie" has made some large investments.

I hope to hear from you soon and that you are enjoying every minute. With much love,

Your friend,

Elinore Stewart.

14

The New House

December 1, 1911.

Dear Mrs. Coney,—

I feel just like visiting tonight, so I am going to "play like" you have
come. It is so good to have you to chat with. Please be seated in this
low rocker; it is a present to me from the Pattersons and I am very
proud of it. I am just back from the Patterson ranch, and they have
a dear little boy who came the 20th of November and they call him
Robert Lane.

I am sure this room must look familiar to you, for there is so much
in it that was once yours. I have two rooms, each fifteen by fifteen, but
this one on the south is my "really" room and in it are my treasures.
My house faces east and is built up against a side-hill, or should I say
hillside? Anyway, they had to excavate quite a lot. I had them dump
the dirt right before the house and terrace it smoothly. I have sown
my terrace to California poppies, and around my porch, which is six
feet wide and thirty long, I have planted wild cucumbers.

Every log in my house is as straight as a pine can grow. Each room
has a window and a door on the east side, and the south room has two
windows on the south with space between for my heater, which is
one of those with a grate front so I can see the fire burn. It is almost
as good as a fireplace. The logs are unhewed outside because I like the
rough finish, but inside the walls are perfectly square and smooth. The
cracks in the walls are snugly filled with "daubing" and then the walls
are covered with heavy gray building-paper, which makes the room
very warm, and I really like the appearance. I had two rolls of wallpaper with a bold rose pattern. By being very careful I was able to cut
out enough of the roses, which are divided in their choice of colour as
to whether they should be red, yellow, or pink, to make a border about

71

THE STEWART CABIN

eighteen inches from the ceiling. They brighten up the wall and the gray paper is fine to hang pictures upon. Those you have sent us make our room very attractive. The woodwork is stained a walnut brown, oil finish, and the floor is stained and oiled just like it. In the corners by the stove and before the windows we take our comfort.

From some broken bamboo fishing-rods I made frames for two screens. These I painted black with some paint that was left from the buggy, and Gavotte fixed the screens so they will stay balanced, and put in casters for me. I had a piece of blue curtain calico and with brass-headed tacks I put it on the frame of Jerrine's screen, then I mixed some paste and let her decorate it to suit herself on the side that should be next her corner. She used the cards you sent her. Some of the people have a suspiciously tottering appearance, perhaps not so very artistic, but they all mean something to a little girl whose small fingers worked patiently to attain satisfactory results. She has a set of shelves on which her treasures of china are arranged. On the floor is a rug made of two goatskins dyed black, a present from Gavotte, who heard her admiring Zebbie's bearskin. She has a tiny red rocking-chair which she has outgrown, but her rather dilapidated family of dolls use it for an automobile. For a seat for herself she has a small hassock that you gave me, and behind the blue screen is a world apart.

My screen is made just like Jerrine's except that the cover is cream material with sprays of wild roses over it. In my corner I have a cot made up like a couch. One of my pillows is covered with some checked gingham that "Dawsie" cross-stitched for me. I have a cabinet bookcase made from an old walnut bedstead that was a relic of the Mountain Meadow Massacre. Gavotte made it for me. In it I have my few books, some odds and ends of china, all gifts, and a few fossil curios. For a floor-covering I have a braided rug of blue and white, made from old sheets and Jerrine's old dresses. In the centre of my room is a square table made of pine and stained brown.

Over it is a table-cover that you gave me. Against the wall near my bed is my "dresser." It is a box with shelves and is covered with the same material as my screen. Above it I have a mirror, but it makes ugly faces at me every time I look into it. Upon the wall near by is a match-holder that you gave me. It is the heads of two fisher-folk. The man has lost his nose, but the old lady still thrusts out her tongue. The material on my screen and "dresser" I bought for curtains, then decided to use some white crossbar I had. But I wish I had not, for every time I look at them I think of poor little Mary Ann Parker.

I am going to make you a cup of tea and wonder if you will see anything familiar about the teapot. You should, I think, for it is another of your many gifts to me. Now I feel that you have a fairly good idea of what my house looks like, on the inside anyway. The magazines and Jerrine's cards and Mother Goose book came long ago, and Jerrine and I were both made happy. I wish I could do nice things for you, but all I can do is to love you.

Your sincere friend,

Elinore Rupert.

15

The "Stocking-Leg" Dinner

February, 1912.

Dear Mrs. Coney,—

. . . . This time I want to tell you about a "stocking-leg" dinner which I attended not long ago. It doesn't sound very respectable, but it was one of the happiest events I ever remember.

Mrs. Louderer was here visiting us, and one afternoon we were all in the kitchen when Gavotte came skimming along on the first pair of snowshoes I ever saw. We have had lots of snow this winter, and many of the hollows and gullies are packed full. Gavotte had no difficulty in coming, and he had come for the mail and to invite us to a feast of "ze hose." I could not think what kind of a dinner it could be, and I did not believe that Mr. Stewart would go, but after Gavotte had explained how much easier it was now than at any other time because the hard-packed snow made it possible to go with bobsleds, I knew he would go. I can't say I really wanted to go, but Mrs. Louderer took it for granted that it would be delightful, so she and Mr. Stewart did the planning. Next morning Gavotte met Mrs. O'Shaughnessy and invited her. Then, taking the mail, he went on ahead to blaze a trail we should follow with the sleds.

We were to start two days later. They planned we could easily make the trip in a day, as, with the gulches filled with snow, short cuts were possible, and we could travel at a good pace, as we would have a strong team. To me it seemed dangerous, but dinner-parties have not been so plenty that I could miss one. So, when the day came on which we were to start, we were up betimes and had a mess-box packed and Mr. Stewart had a big pile of rocks hot. We all wore our warmest clothes, and the rest carried out hot rocks and blankets while I put the kitchen in such order that the men left to feed the stock would have no trouble in getting their meals. Mr. Stewart carried out the mess-box, and presently we were off. We had a wagon-box on bobsleds, and the box was filled with hay and hot rocks with blankets on top and more to cover us. Mr. Stewart had two big bags of grain in front, feed for the horses, and he sat on them.

It was a beautiful day and we jogged along merrily. We had lots of fun, and as we went a new way, there was much that was new to Mrs. O'Shaughnessy and myself, and it was all new to the rest. Gavotte had told us where we should noon, and we reached the place shortly after twelve. Mr. Stewart went to lift out the mess-box,—but he had forgotten to put it in! Oh, dear! We were a disappointed lot. I don't think I was ever so hungry, but there was nothing for it but to grin and bear it. It did me some good, though, to remember how a man misses his dinner. The horses had to be fed, so we walked about while they were eating. We went up a *cañon* that had high cliffs on one side, and came to a place where, high up on the rock wall, in great black letters, was this legend: "Dick fell off of this here clift and died." I should think there would be no question that anyone who fell from that place on to the boulders below *would* die.

Soon we started again, and if not quite so jolly as we were before, at least we looked forward to our supper with a keen relish and the horses were urged faster than they otherwise would have been. The beautiful snow is rather depressing, however, when there is snow everywhere. The afternoon passed swiftly and the horses were becoming jaded. At four o'clock it was almost dark. We had been going up a deep *cañon* and came upon an appalling sight. There had been a snow-slide and the *cañon* was half-filled with snow, rock, and broken trees. The whole way was blocked, and what to do we didn't know, for the horses could hardly be gotten along and we could not pass the snow-slide. We were twenty-five miles from home, night was almost upon us, and we were almost starved. But we were afraid to stay in that *cañon* lest more snow should slide and bury us, so sadly we turned back to find as comfortable a place as we could to spend the night.

The prospects were very discouraging, and I am afraid we were all near tears, when suddenly there came upon the cold air a clear blast from a horn. Mrs. Louderer cried, "*Ach, der reveille!*" Once I heard a lecturer tell of climbing the Matterhorn and the calls we heard brought his story to mind. No music could have been so beautiful. It soon became apparent that we were being signalled; so we drove in the direction of the sound and found ourselves going up a wide *cañon*.

We had passed the mouth of it shortly before we had come to the slide. Even the tired horses took new courage, and every few moments a sweet, clear call put new heart into us. Soon we saw a light. We had to drive very slowly and in places barely crept. The bugler changed his notes and we knew he was wondering if we were coming, so Mr. Stewart helloed. At once we had an answer, and after that we were steadily guided by the horn. Many times we could not see the light, but we drove in the right direction because we could hear the horn.

At last, when it was quite dark and the horses could go no farther, we drew up before the fire that had been our beacon light. It was a bonfire built out upon a point of rock at the end of the *cañon*. Back from it among the pines was a *'dobe* house. A dried-up mummy of a man advanced from the fire to meet us, explaining that he had seen us through his field-glasses and, knowing about the snow-slide, had ventured to attract us to his poor place. Carlota Juanita was within, prepared for the *señoras*, if they would but walk in. If they would! More dead than alive, we scrambled out, cold-stiffened and hungry. Carlota Juanita threw open the low, wide door and we stumbled into comfort. She hastened to help us off with our wraps, piled more wood on the open fire, and busied herself to make us welcome and comfortable. Poor Carlota Juanita!

Perhaps you think she was some slender, limpid-eyed, olive-cheeked beauty. She was fat and forty, but not fair. She had the biggest wad of hair that I ever saw, and her face was so fat that her eyes looked beady. She wore an old heelless pair of slippers or sandals that would hardly stay on, and at every step they made the most exasperating sliding noise, but she was all kindness and made us feel very welcome. The floor was of dirt, and they had the largest fireplace I have ever seen, with the widest, cleanest hearth, which was where they did their cooking. All their furniture was home-made, and on a low bench near the door were three water-jars which, I am sure, were handmade. Away back in a corner they had a small altar, on which was a little statue of Mary and the Child. Before it, suspended by a wire from the rafters, was a cow's horn in which a piece of punk was burning, just as the incense is kept burning in churches.

Supper was already prepared and was simmering and smoking on the hearth. As soon as the men came in, Carlota Juanita put it on the table, which was bare of cloth. I can't say that I really like Mexican bread, but they certainly know how to cook meat. They had a most wonderful pot-roast with potatoes and corn dumplings that were delicious. The roast had been slashed in places and small bits of garlic, pepper, bacon, and, I think, parsley, inserted. After it and the potatoes and the dumplings were done, Carlota had poured in a can of tomatoes. You may not think that was good, but I can assure you it was and that we did ample justice to it.

After we had eaten until we were hardly able to swallow, Carlota Juanita served a queer Mexican pie. It was made of dried buffalo-berries, stewed and made very sweet. A layer of batter had been poured into a deep baking-dish, then the berries, and then more batter. Then it was baked and served hot with plenty of hard sauce; and it was powerful good, too. She had very peculiar coffee with goat's milk in it. I took mine without the milk, but I couldn't make up my mind that I liked the coffee.

We sat around the fire drinking it, when Manuel Pedro Felipe told us it was some he had brought from Mexico. I didn't know they raised it there, but he told us many interesting things about it. He and Carlota Juanita both spoke fairly good English. They had lived for many years in their present home and had some sheep, a few goats, a cow or two, a few pigs, and chickens and turkeys. They had a small patch of land that Carlota Juanita tilled and on which was raised the squaw corn that hung in bunches from the rafters. Down where we live we can't get sweet corn to mature, but here, so much higher up, they have a sheltered little nook where they are able to raise many things. Upon a long shelf above the fire was an ugly old stone image, the bottom broken off and some plaster applied to make it set level.

The ugly thing they had brought with them from some old ruined temple in Mexico. We were all so very tired that soon Carlota Juanita brought out an armful of the thickest, brightest rugs and spread them over the floor for us to sleep upon. The men retired to a lean-to room, where they slept, but not before Manuel Pedro Felipe and Carlota had knelt before their altar for their devotions. Mrs. O'Shaughnessy and myself and Jerrine, knowing the rosary, surprised them by kneeling with them. It is good to meet with kindred faith away off in the mountains.

It seems there could not possibly be a mistake when people so far away from creeds and doctrines hold to the faith of their childhood and find the practice a pleasure after so many years. The men bade us goodnight, and we lost no time in settling ourselves to rest. Luckily we had plenty of blankets.

Away in the night I was awakened by a noise that frightened me.

All was still, but instantly there flashed through my mind tales of murdered travellers, and I was almost paralyzed with fear when again I heard that stealthy, sliding noise, just like Carlota Juanita's old slippers. The fire had burned down, but just then the moon came from behind a cloud and shone through the window upon Carlota Juanita, who was asleep with her mouth open. I could also see a pine bough which was scraping against the wall outside, which was perhaps making the noise. I turned over and saw the punk burning, which cast a dim light over the serene face of the Blessed Virgin, so all fear vanished and I slept as long as they would let me in the morning.

After a breakfast of *tortillas*, cheese, and rancid butter, and some more of the coffee, we started again for the stocking-leg dinner. Carlota Juanita stood in the door, waving to us as long as we could see her, and Manuel P.F. sat with Mr. Stewart to guide us around the snow-slide. Under one arm he carried the horn with which he had called us to him. It came from some long-horned cow in Mexico, was beautifully polished, and had a fancy rim of silver. I should like to own it, but I could not make it produce a sound. When we were safe on our way our guide left us, and our spirits ran high again. The horses were feeling good also, so it was a merry, laughing party that drew up before Zebbie's two hours later.

Long before I had lent Gavotte a set of the *Leather-Stocking Tales*, which he had read aloud to Zebbie. Together they had planned a Leather-Stocking dinner, at which should be served as many of the viands mentioned in the *Tales* as possible. We stayed two days and it was one long feast. We had venison served in half a dozen different ways. We had antelope; we had porcupine, or hedgehog, as Pathfinder called it; and also we had beaver-tail, which he found toothsome, but which I did *not*. We had grouse and sage hen. They broke the ice and snared a lot of trout. In their cellar they had a barrel of trout prepared exactly like mackerel, and they were more delicious than mackerel because they were finer-grained. I had been a little disappointed in Zebbie after his return from home. It seemed to me that Pauline had spoiled him. I guess I was jealous. This time he was the same little old Zebbie I had first seen. He seemed to thoroughly enjoy our visit, and I am sure we each had the time of our lives. We made it home without mishap the same day we started, all of us sure life held something new and enjoyable after all.

If nothing happens there are some more good times in store for me this summer. Gavotte once worked under Professor Marsden when he was out here getting fossils for the Smithsonian Institution, and he is very interesting to listen to. He has invited us to go with him out to the Bad-Land hills in the summer to search for fossils. The hills are only a few miles from here and I look forward to a splendid time.

16

The Horse-Thieves

Dear Mrs. Coney,—

. . . . I am so afraid that you will get an overdose of culture from your visit to the Hub and am sending you an antidote of our sage, sand, and sunshine.

Mrs. Louderer had come over to see our boy. Together we had prepared supper and were waiting for Clyde, who had gone to the post-office. Soon he came, and after the usual friendly wrangling between him and Mrs. Louderer we had supper. Then they began their inevitable game of cribbage, while I sat near the fire with baby on my lap. Clyde was telling us of a raid on a ranch about seventy-five miles away, in which the thieves had driven off thirty head of fine horses. There were only two of the thieves, and the sheriff with a large posse was pursuing them and forcing every man they came across into the chase, and a regular man-hunt was on. It was interesting only because one of the thieves was a noted outlaw then out on parole and known to be desperate. We were in no way alarmed; the trouble was all in the next county, and somehow that always seems so far away. We knew if the men ever came together there would be a pitched battle, with bloodshed and death, but there seemed little chance that the sheriff would ever overtake the men.

I remember I was feeling sorry for the poor fellows with a price on their heads,—the little pink man on my lap had softened my heart wonderfully. Jerrine was enjoying the pictures in a paper illustrating early days on the range, wild scenes of roping and branding. I had remarked that I didn't believe there were any more such times, when Mrs Louderer replied, "Dot yust shows how much it iss you do not know. You shall come to mine house and when away you come it shall be wiser as when you left." I had kept at home very closely all summer, and a little trip seemed the most desirable thing I could think of, particularly as the baby would be in no way endangered. But long ago I learned that the quickest way to get what I want is not to want it, outwardly, at least. So I assumed an indifference that was not very real. The result was that next morning every one was in a hurry to get me started,—Clyde greasing the little old wagon that looks like a twin to Cora Belle's, and Mrs. Louderer, who thinks no baby can be properly brought up without goose-grease, busy greasing the baby "so as he shall not some cold take yet." Mrs. Louderer had ridden over, so her saddle was laid in the wagon and her pony, Bismarck, was hitched in with Chub, the laziest horse in all Wyoming. I knew Clyde could manage very well while I should be gone, and there wasn't a worry to interfere with the pleasure of my outing.

We jogged along right merrily, Mrs. Louderer devoting her entire attention to trying to make Chub pull even with Bismarck, Jerrine and myself enjoying the ever-changing views. I wish I could lay it all before you. Summer was departing with reluctant feet, unafraid of Winter's messengers, the chill winds. That day was especially beautiful. The gleaming snow peaks and heavy forest south and at our back; west, north, and east, long, broken lines of the distant mountains with their blue haze. Pilot Butte to the north, one hundred miles away, stood out clear and distinct as though we could drive there in an hour or two. The dull, neutral-coloured "Bad Land" hills nearer us are interesting only because we know they are full of the fossil remains of strange creatures long since extinct.

For a distance our way lay up Henry's Fork valley; prosperous little ranches dotted the view, ripening grain rustled pleasantly in the warm morning sunshine, and closely cut alfalfa fields made bright spots of emerald against the dun landscape. The quaking aspens were just beginning to turn yellow; everywhere purple asters were a blaze of glory except where the rabbit-bush grew in clumps, waving its feathery plumes of gold. Over it all the sky was so deeply blue, with little, airy, white clouds drifting lazily along. Every breeze brought scents of cedar, pine, and sage. At this point the road wound along the base of cedar hills; some magpies were holding a noisy caucus among the trees, a pair of bluebirds twittered excitedly upon a fence, and high overhead a great black eagle soared. All was so peaceful that horse-thieves and desperate men seemed too remote to think about.

Presently we crossed the creek and headed our course due north toward the desert and the buttes. I saw that we were not going right to reach Mrs. Louderer's ranch, so I asked where we were supposed to be going. "We iss going to the mouth of Dry Creek by, where it goes Black's Fork into. Dere mine punchers holdts five huntert steers. We shall de camp visit and you shall come back wiser as when you went."

Well, we both came away wiser. I had thought we were going only to the Louderer ranch, so I put up no lunch, and there was nothing for the horses either. But it was too beautiful a time to let such things annoy us. Anyway, we expected to reach camp just after noon, so a little delay about dinner didn't seem so bad. We had entered the desert by noon; the warm, red sands fell away from the wheels with soft, hissing sounds. Occasionally a little horned toad sped panting along before us, suddenly darting aside to watch with bright, cunning eyes as we passed. Someone had placed a buffalo's skull beside a big bunch of sage and on the sage a splendid pair of elk's antlers. We saw many such scattered over the sands, grim reminders of a past forever gone.

About three o'clock we reached our destination, but no camp was there. We were more disappointed than I can tell you, but Mrs. Louderer merely went down to the river, a few yards away, and cut an armful of willow sticks wherewith to coax Chub to a little brisker pace, and then we took the trail of the departed mess-wagon. Shortly, we topped a low range of hills, and beyond, in a cuplike valley, was the herd of sleek beauties feeding contentedly on the lush green grass. I suppose it sounds odd to hear desert and river in the same breath, but within a few feet of the river the desert begins, where nothing grows but sage and greasewood. In oasis-like spots will be found plenty of grass where the soil is nearer the surface and where sub-irrigation keeps the roots watered. In one of these spots the herd was being held. When the grass became short they would be moved to another such place.

It required, altogether, fifteen men to take care of the herd, because many of the cattle had been bought in different places, some in Utah, and these were always trying to run away and work back toward home, so they required constant herding. Soon we caught the glimmer of white canvas, and knew it was the cover of the mess-wagon, so we headed that way.

The camp was quite near the river so as to be handy to water and to have the willows for wood. Not a soul was at camp. The fire was out, and even the ashes had blown away. The mess-box was locked and Mrs. Louderer's loud calls brought only echoes from the high rock walls across the river. However, there was nothing to do but to make the best of it, so we tethered the horses and went down to the river to relieve ourselves of the dust that seemed determined to unite with the dust that we were made of. Mrs. Louderer declared she was "so mat as nodings and would fire dot Herman so soon as she could see him already."

Presently we saw the most grotesque figure approaching camp. It was Herman, the fat cook, on Hunks, a gaunt, ugly old horse, whose days of usefulness under the saddle were past and who had degenerated into a workhorse. The disgrace of it seemed to be driving him into a decline, but he stumbled along bravely under his heavy load. A string of a dozen sage chickens swung on one side, and across the saddle in front of Herman lay a young antelope. A volley of German abuse was hurled at poor Herman, wound up in as plain American as Mrs. Louderer could speak: "And who iss going to pay de game warden de fine of dot antelope what you haf shot? And how iss it that we haf come de camp by und so starved as we iss hungry, and no cook und no food? Iss dat for why you iss paid?"

Herman was some Dutch himself, however. "How iss it," he demanded, "dat you haf not so much sense as you haf tongue? How haf you lived so long as always in de West und don't know enough to hunt a bean-hole when you reach your own camp. Hey?"

Mrs. Louderer was very properly subdued and I delighted when he removed the stones from where the fire had been, exposing a pit from which, with a pair of pot-hooks, he lifted pots and ovens of the most delicious meat, beans, and potatoes. From the mess-box he brought bread and apricot pie. From a near-by spring he brought us a bright, new pail full of clear, sparkling water, but Mrs. Louderer insisted upon tea and in a short time he had it ready for us. The tarpaulin was spread on the ground for us to eat from, and soon we were showing an astonished cook just how much food two women and a child could get away with. I ate a good deal of ashes with my roast beef and we all ate more or less sand, but fastidiousness about food is a good thing to get rid of when you come West to camp.

When the regular supper-time arrived the punchers began to gather in, and the "boss," who had been to town about some business, came in and brought back the news of the man-hunt. The punchers sat about the fire, eating hungrily from their tin plates and eagerly listening to the recital. Two of the boys were tenderfeet: one from

Tennessee called "Daisy Belle," because he whistled that tune so much and because he had nose-bleed so much,—couldn't even ride a broncho but his nose would bleed for hours afterwards; and the other, "N'Yawk," so called from his native State. N'Yawk was a great boaster; said he wasn't afraid of no durned outlaw,—said his father had waded in bloody gore up to his neck and that he was a chip off the old block,—rather hoped the chase would come our way so he could try his marksmanship.

The air began to grow chill and the sky was becoming overcast. Preparations for the night busied everybody. Fresh ponies were being saddled for the night relief, the hard-ridden, tired ones that had been used that day being turned loose to graze. Some poles were set up and a tarpaulin arranged for Mrs. Louderer and me to sleep under. Mrs. Louderer and Jerrine lay down on some blankets and I unrolled some more, which I was glad to notice were clean, for Baby and myself. I can't remember ever being more tired and sleepy, but I couldn't go to sleep. I could hear the boss giving orders in quick, decisive tones. I could hear the punchers discussing the raid, finally each of them telling exploits of his favourite heroes of outlawry. I could hear Herman, busy among his pots and pans. Then he mounted the tongue of the mess-wagon and called out, "We haf for breakfast cackle-berries, first vot iss come iss served, und those vot iss sleep late gets nodings."

I had never before heard of cackle-berries and asked sleepy Mrs. Louderer what they were. "Vait until morning and you shall see," was all the information that I received.

Soon a gentle, drizzling rain began, and the punchers hurriedly made their beds, as they did so twitting N'Yawk about making his between our tent and the fire. "You're dead right, pard," I heard one of them say, "to make your bed there, fer if them outlaws comes this way they'll think you air one of the women and they won't shoot you. Just us *men* air in danger."

"Confound your fool tongues, how they goin' to know there's any women here? I tell you, fellers, my old man waded in bloody gore up to his neck and I'm just like him."

They kept up this friendly parleying until I dozed off to sleep, but I couldn't stay asleep. I don't think I was afraid, but I certainly was nervous. The river was making a sad, moaning sound; the rain fell gently, like tears. All nature seemed to be mourning about something, happened or going to happen. Down by the river an owl hooted dismally. Half a mile away the night-herders were riding round and round the herd. One of them was singing,—faint but distinct came his song: "Bury me not on the lone prairie." Over and over again he sang it. After a short interval of silence he began again. This time it was, "I'm thinking of my dear old mother, ten thousand miles away."

Two punchers stirred uneasily and began talking. "Blast that Tex," I heard one of them say, "he certainly has it bad tonight. What the deuce makes him sing so much? I feel like bawling like a kid; I wish he'd shut up."

"He's homesick; I guess we all are too, but they ain't no use staying awake and letting it soak in. Shake the water off the tarp, you air lettin' water catch on your side an' it's running into my ear."

That is the last I heard for a long time. I must have slept. I remember that the baby stirred and I spoke to him. It seemed to me that something struck against the guy-rope that held our tarpaulin taut, but I wasn't sure. I was in that dozy state, half asleep, when nothing is quite clear. It seemed as though I had been listening to the tramp of feet for hours and that a whole army must be filing past, when I was brought suddenly into keen consciousness by a loud voice demanding, "Hello! Whose outfit is this?"

"This is the 7 Up,—Louderer's," the boss called back; "what's wanted?"

"Is that you, Mat? This is Ward's posse. We been after Meeks and Murdock all night. It's so durned dark we can't see, but we got to keep going; their horses are about played. We changed at Hadley's, but we ain't had a bite to eat and we got to search your camp."

"Sure thing," the boss answered, "roll off and take a look. Hi, there, you Herm, get out of there and fix these fellers something to eat."

We were surrounded. I could hear the clanking of spurs and the sound of the wet, tired horses shaking themselves and rattling the saddles on every side. "Who's in the wickiup?" I heard the sheriff ask.

"Some women and kids,—Mrs. Louderer and a friend."

In an incredibly short time Herman had a fire coaxed into a blaze and Mat Watson and the sheriff went from bed to bed with a lantern. They searched the mess-wagon, even, although Herman had been sleeping there. The sheriff unceremoniously flung out the wood and kindling the cook had stored there. He threw back the flap of our tent and flashed the lantern about. He could see plainly enough that there were but the four of us, but I wondered how they saw outside where the rain made it worse, the lantern was so dirty. "Yes," I heard the sheriff say, "we've been pushing them hard. They're headed north, evidently intend to hit the railroad but they'll never make it. Every ford on the river is guarded except right along here, and there's five parties ranging on the other side. My party's split,—a bunch has gone on to the bridge. If they find anything they're to fire a volley. Same with us. I knew they couldn't cross the river nowhere but at the bridge or here."

The men had gathered about the fire and were gulping hot coffee and cold beef and bread. The rain ran off their slickers in little rivulets. I was sorry the fire was not better, because some of the men had on only ordinary coats, and the drizzling rain seemed determined that the fire should not blaze high.

Before they had finished eating we heard a shot, followed by a regular medley of dull booms. The men were in their saddles and gone in less time than it takes to tell it. The firing had ceased save for a few sharp reports from the revolvers, like a coyote's spiteful snapping. The pounding of the horse's hoofs grew fainter, and soon all was still. I kept my ears strained for the slightest sound. The cook and the boss, the only men up, hurried back to bed. Watson had risen so hurriedly that he had not been careful about his "tarp" and water had run into his bed. But that wouldn't disconcert anybody but a tenderfoot. I kept waiting in tense silence to hear them come back with dead or wounded, but there was not a sound. The rain had stopped. Mrs. Louderer struck a match and said it was three o'clock. Soon she was asleep. Through a rift in the clouds a star peeped out. I could smell the wet sage and the sand. A little breeze came by, bringing Tex's song once more:—

Oh, it matters not, so I've been told,
How the body lies when the heart grows cold.

Oh, dear! the world seemed so full of sadness. I kissed my baby's little downy head and went to sleep.

It seems that cowboys are rather sleepy-headed in the morning and it is a part of the cook's job to get them up. The next I knew, Herman had a tin pan on which he was beating a vigorous tattoo, all the time hollering, "We haf cackle-berries *und* antelope steak for breakfast." The baby was startled by the noise, so I attended to him and then dressed myself for breakfast. I went down to the little spring to wash my face. The morning was lowering and gray, but a wind had sprung up and the clouds were parting. There are times when anticipation is a great deal better than realisation. Never having seen a cackle-berry, my imagination pictured them as some very luscious wild fruit, and I was so afraid none would be left that I couldn't wait until the men should eat and be gone. So I surprised them by joining the very earliest about the fire. Herman began serving breakfast. I held out my tin plate and received some of the steak, an egg, and two delicious biscuits. We had our coffee in big enameled cups, without sugar or cream, but it was piping hot and *so* good. I had finished my egg and steak and so I told Herman I was ready for my cackle-berries.

"Listen to her now, will you?" he asked. And then indignantly, "How many cackle-berries does you want? You haf had so many as I haf cooked for you."

"Why, Herman, I haven't had a single berry," I said.

Then such a roar of laughter. Herman gazed at me in astonishment, and Mr. Watson gently explained to me that eggs and cackle-berries were one and the same.

N'Yawk was not yet up, so Herman walked over to his bed, kicked him a few times, and told him he would scald him if he didn't turn out. It was quite light by then. N'Yawk joined us in a few minutes. "What the deuce was you fellers kicking up such a rumpus fer last night?" he asked.

"You blamed blockhead, don't you know?" the boss answered. "Why, the sheriff searched this camp last night. They had a battle down at the bridge afterwards and either they are all killed or else no one is hurt. They would have been here otherwise. Ward took a shot at them once yesterday, but I guess he didn't hit; the men got away, anyway. And durn your sleepy head! you just lay there and snored. Well, I'll be danged!" Words failed him, his wonder and disgust were so great.

N'Yawk turned to get his breakfast. His light shirt was blood-stained in the back,—seemed to be soaked. "What's the matter with your shirt, it's soaked with blood?" someone asked.

"Then that durned Daisy Belle has been crawling in with me, that's all," he said. "Blame his bleeding snoot. I'll punch it and give it something to bleed for."

Then Mr. Watson said, "Daisy ain't been in all night. He took Jesse's place when he went to town after supper." That started an inquiry and search which speedily showed that some one with a bleeding wound had gotten in with N'Yawk. It also developed that Mr. Watson's splendid horse and saddle were gone, the rope that the horse had been picketed with lying just as it had been cut from his neck.

Now all was bustle and excitement. It was plainly evident that one of the outlaws had lain hidden on N'Yawk's bed while the sheriff was there, and that afterwards he had saddled the horse and made his escape. His own horse was found in the willows, the saddle cut loose and the bridle off, but the poor, jaded thing had never moved. By sunup the search-party returned, all too worn-out with twenty-four hours in the saddle to continue the hunt. They were even too worn-out to eat, but flung themselves down for a few hours' rest. The chase was hopeless anyway, for the search-party had gone north in the night. The wounded outlaw had doubtless heard the sheriff talking and, the coast being clear to the southward, had got the fresh horse and was by that time probably safe in the heavy forests and mountains of Utah. His getting in with N'Yawk had been a daring ruse, but a successful one. Where his partner was, no one could guess. But by that time all the camp excepting Herman and Mrs. Louderer were so panicky that we couldn't have made a rational suggestion.

N'Yawk, white around his mouth, approached Mrs. Louderer. "I want to quit," he said.

"Well," she said, calmly sipping her coffee, "you haf done it."

"I'm sick," he stammered.

"I know you iss," she said, "I haf before now seen men get sick when they iss scared to death."

"My old daddy—" he began.

"Yes, I know, he waded the creek vone time und you has had cold feet effer since."

Poor fellow, I felt sorry for him. I had cold feet myself just then, and I was powerfully anxious to warm them by my own fire where a pair of calm blue eyes would reassure me.

I didn't get to see the branding that was to have taken place on the range that day. The boss insisted on taking the trail of his valued horse. He was very angry. He thought there was a traitor among the posse. Who started the firing at the bridge no one knew, and Watson said openly that it was done to get the sheriff away from camp.

My own home looked mighty good to me when we drove up that evening. I don't want any more wild life on the range,—not for a while, anyway.

Your ex-Washlady,

Elinore Rupert Stewart.

17

At Gavotte's Camp

November 16, 1912.

My dear Friend,—

At last I can write you as I want to. I am afraid you think I am going to wait until the "bairns" are grown up before writing to my friends, but indeed I shall not. I fully intend to "*gather roses while I may.*" Since God has given me two blessings, children and friends, I shall enjoy them both as I go along.

I must tell you why I have not written as I should have done. All summer long my eyes were so strained and painful that I had to let all reading and writing go. And I have suffered terribly with my back. But now I am able to be about again, do most of my own work, and my eyes are much better. So now I shall not treat you so badly again. If you could only know how kind every one is to me, you would know that even ill health has its compensations out here. Dear Mrs. Louderer, with her goose-grease, her bread, and her delicious "kuchens." Mrs. O'Shaughnessy, with her cheery ways, her tireless friendship, and willing, capable hands. Gavotte even, with his tidbits of game and fish. Dear little Cora Belle came often to see me, sometimes bringing me a little of Grandpa's latest cure, which I received on faith, for, of course, I could not really swallow any of it. Zebbie's nephew, Parker Carter, came out, spent the summer with him, and they have now gone back to Yell County, leaving Gavotte in charge again.

Gavotte had a most interesting and prosperous summer. He was commissioned by a wealthy Easterner to procure some fossils. I had had such a confined summer that Clyde took me out to Gavotte's camp as soon as I was able to sit up and be driven. We found him away over in the bad lands camped in a fine little grove. He is a charming man to visit at any time, and we found him in a particularly happy

GAVOTTE

mood. He had just begun to quarry a gigantic find; he had piles of specimens; he had packed and shipped some rare specimens of fossil plants, but his "beeg find" came later and he was jubilant. To dig fossils successfully requires great care and knowledge, but it is a work in which Gavotte excels. He is a splendid cook. I almost believe he could make a Johnny Reb like codfish, and that night we had a delicious supper and all the time listening to a learned discourse about prehistoric things. I enjoyed the meal and I enjoyed the talk, but I could not sleep peacefully for being chased in my dreams by pterodactyls, dinosaurs, and iguanodons, besides a great many horrible creatures whose names I have forgotten. Of course, when the ground begins to freeze and snow comes, fossil-mining is done for until summer comes, so Gavotte tends the critters and traps this winter. I shall not get to go to the mountains this winter. The babies are too small, but there is always some happy and interesting thing happening, and I shall have two pleasures each time, my own enjoyment, and getting to tell you of them.

18

The Homesteader's Marriage and a Little Funeral

Dear Mrs. Coney,—

Every time I get a new letter from you I get a new inspiration, and I am always glad to hear from you.

I have often wished I might tell you all about my Clyde, but have not because of two things. One is I could not even begin without telling you what a good man he is, and I didn't want you to think I could do nothing but brag. The other reason is the haste I married in. I am ashamed of that. I am afraid you will think me a Becky Sharp of a person. But although I married in haste, I have no cause to repent. That is very fortunate because I have never had one bit of leisure to repent in. So I am lucky all around. The engagement was powerfully short because both agreed that the trend of events and ranch work seemed to require that we be married first and do our "sparking" afterward. You see, we had to chink in the wedding between times, that is, between planting the oats and other work that must be done early or not at all. In Wyoming ranchers can scarcely take time even to be married in the springtime.

That having been settled, the license was sent for by mail, and as soon as it came Mr. Stewart saddled Chub and went down to the house of Mr. Pearson, the justice of the peace and a friend of long standing. I had never met any of the family and naturally rather dreaded to have them come, but Mr. Stewart was firm in wanting to be married at home, so he told Mr. Pearson he wanted him and his family to come up the following Wednesday and serve papers on the "wooman i' the hoose." They were astonished, of course, but being such good friends they promised him all the assistance they could render. They are quite the dearest, most interesting family! I have since learned to love them as my own.

Well, there was no time to make wedding clothes, so I had to "do up" what I did have. Isn't it queer how sometimes, do what you can, work will keep getting in the way until you can't get anything done? That is how it was with me those few days before the wedding; so much so that when Wednesday dawned everything was topsy-turvy and I had a very strong desire to run away. But I always did hate a "piker," so I stood pat. Well, I had most of the dinner cooked, but it kept me hustling to get the house into anything like decent order before the old dog barked, and I knew my moments of liberty were limited. It was blowing a perfect hurricane and snowing like midwinter. I had bought a beautiful pair of shoes to wear on that day, but my vanity had squeezed my feet a little, so while I was so busy at work I had kept on a worn old pair, intending to put on the new ones later; but when the Pearsons drove up all I thought about was getting them into the house where there was fire, so I forgot all about the old shoes and the apron I wore.

I had only been here six weeks then, and was a stranger. That is why I had no one to help me and was so confused and hurried. As soon as the newcomers were warm, Mr. Stewart told me I had better come over by him and stand up. It was a large room I had to cross, and how I did it before all those strange eyes I never knew. All I can remember very distinctly is hearing Mr. Stewart saying, "I will," and myself chiming in that I would, too. Happening to glance down, I saw that I had forgotten to take off my apron or my old shoes, but just then Mr. Pearson pronounced us man and wife, and as I had dinner to serve right away I had no time to worry over my odd toilet. Anyway the shoes were comfortable and the apron white, so I suppose it could have been worse; and I don't think it has ever made any difference with the Pearsons, for I number them all among my most esteemed friends.

It is customary here for newlyweds to give a dance and supper at the hall, but as I was a stranger I preferred not to, and so it was a long time before I became acquainted with all my neighbours. I had not thought I should ever marry again. Jerrine was always such a dear little pal, and I wanted to just knock about foot-loose and free to see life as a gypsy sees it. I had planned to see the Cliff-Dwellers' home; to live right there until I caught the spirit of the surroundings enough to live over their lives in imagination anyway. I had planned to see the old missions and to go to Alaska; to hunt in Canada. I even dreamed of Honolulu. Life stretched out before me one long, happy jaunt. I aimed to see all the world I could, but to travel unknown bypaths to do it. But first I wanted to try homesteading.

But for my having the grippe, I should never have come to Wyoming. Mrs. Seroise, who was a nurse at the institution for nurses in Denver while I was housekeeper there, had worked one summer at Saratoga, Wyoming. It was she who told me of the pine forests. I had never seen a pine until I came to Colorado; so the idea of a home among the pines fascinated me. At that time I was hoping to pass the Civil-Service examination, with no very definite idea as to what I would do, but just to be improving my time and opportunity. I never went to a public school a day in my life. In my childhood days there was no such thing in the Indian Territory part of Oklahoma where we lived, so I have had to try hard to keep learning. Before the time came for the examination I was so discouraged because of the grippe that nothing but the mountains, the pines, and the clean, fresh air seemed worth while; so it all came about just as I have written you.

So you see I was very deceitful. Do you remember, I wrote you of a little baby boy dying? That was my own little Jamie, our first little son. For a long time my heart was crushed. He was such a sweet, beautiful boy. I wanted him so much. He died of *erysipelas*. I held him in my arms till the last agony was over. Then I dressed the beautiful little body for the grave. Clyde is a carpenter; so I wanted him to make the little coffin. He did it every bit, and I lined and padded it, trimmed and covered it. Not that we couldn't afford to buy one or that our neighbours were not all that was kind and willing; but because it was a sad pleasure to do everything for our little first-born ourselves.

As there had been no physician to help, so there was no minister to comfort, and I could not bear to let our baby leave the world without leaving any message to a community that sadly needed it. His little message to us had been love, so I selected a chapter from John and we had a funeral service, at which all our neighbours for thirty miles around were present. So you see, our union is sealed by love and welded by a great sorrow.

Little Jamie was the first little Stewart. God has given me two more precious little sons. The old sorrow is not so keen now. I can bear to tell you about it, but I never could before. When you think of me, you must think of me as one who is truly happy. It is true, I want a great many things I haven't got, but I don't want them enough to be discontented and not enjoy the many blessings that are mine. I have my home among the blue mountains, my healthy, well-formed children, my clean, honest husband, my kind, gentle milk cows, my garden which I make myself. I have loads and loads of flowers which I tend myself. There are lots of chickens, turkeys, and pigs which are my own special care. I have some slow old gentle horses and an old wagon. I can load up the kiddies and go where I please any time. I have the best, kindest neighbours and I have my dear absent friends. Do you wonder I am so happy? When I think of it all, I wonder how I can crowd all my joy into one short life. I don't want you to think for one moment that you are bothering me when I write you. It is a real pleasure to do so. You're always so good to let me tell you everything. I am only afraid of trying your patience too far. Even in this long letter I can't tell you all I want to; so I shall write you again soon. Jerrine will write too. Just now she has very sore fingers. She has been picking gooseberries, and they have been pretty severe on her brown little paws.

With much love to you, I am

"Honest and truly" yours,

Elinore Rupert Stewart.

19

The Adventure of the Christmas Tree

January 6, 1913.

My dear Friend,—

I have put off writing you and thanking you for your thought for us until now so that I could tell you of our very happy Christmas and our deer hunt all at once.

To begin with, Mr. Stewart and Junior have gone to Boulder to spend the winter. Clyde wanted his mother to have a chance to enjoy our boy, so, as he had to go, he took Junior with him. Then those of my dear neighbours nearest my heart decided to prevent a lonely Christmas for me, so on December 21st came Mrs. Louderer, laden with an immense plum pudding and a big "*wurst*," and a little later came Mrs. O'Shaughnessy on her frisky pony, Chief, her scarlet sweater making a bright bit of colour against our snow-wrapped horizon. Her face and ways are just as bright and cheery as can be. When she saw Mrs. Louderer's pudding and sausage she said she had brought nothing because she had come to get something to eat herself, "and," she continued, "it is a private opinion of mine that my neighbours are so glad to see me that they are glad to feed me." Now wouldn't that little speech have made her welcome anywhere?

Well, we were hilariously planning what Mrs. O'Shaughnessy called a "widdy" Christmas and getting supper, when a great stamping-off of snow proclaimed a newcomer. It was Gavotte, and we were powerfully glad to see him because the hired man was going to a dance and we knew Gavotte would contrive some unusual amusement. He had heard that Clyde was going to have a deer-drive, and didn't know that he had gone, so he had come down to join the hunt just for the fun, and was very much disappointed to find there was going to be no hunt. After supper, however, his good humour returned and he told us story after story of big hunts he had had in Canada. He worked up his own enthusiasm as well as ours, and at last proposed that we have a drive of our own for a Christmas "joy." He said he would take a station and do the shooting if one of us would do the driving. So right now I reckon I had better tell you how it is done.

There are many little parks in the mountains where the deer can feed, although now most places are so deep in snow that they can't walk in it. For that reason they have trails to water and to the different feeding-grounds, and they can't get through the snow except along these paths. You see how easy it would be for a man hidden on the trail to get one of the beautiful creatures if some one coming from another direction startled them so that they came along that particular path.

So they made their plans. Mrs. O'Shaughnessy elected herself driver. Two miles away is a huge mountain called Phillipeco, and deer were said to be plentiful up there. At one time there had been a saw-mill on the mountain, and there were a number of deserted cabins in which we could make ourselves comfortable. So it was planned that we go up the next morning, stay all night, have the hunt the following morning, and then come home with our game.

Well, we were all astir early the next morning and soon grain, bedding, and chuck-box were in the wagon. Then Mrs. Louderer, the *kinder*, and myself piled in; Mrs. O'Shaughnessy bestrode Chief, Gavotte stalked on ahead to pick our way, and we were off.

It was a long, tedious climb, and I wished over and over that I had stayed at home; but it was altogether on baby's account. I was so afraid that he would suffer, but he kept warm as toast. The day was beautiful, and the views many times repaid us for any hardship we had suffered. It was three o'clock before we reached the old mill camp. Soon we had a roaring fire, and Gavotte made the horses comfortable in one of the cabins. They were bedded in soft, dry sawdust, and were quite as well off as if they had been in their own stalls. Then some rough planks were laid on blocks, and we had our first meal since breakfast. We called it supper, and we had potatoes roasted in the embers, Mrs. Louderer's *wurst*, which she had been calmly carrying around on her arm like a hoop and which was delicious with the bread that Gavotte toasted on long sticks; we had steaming coffee, and we were all happy; even baby clapped his hands and crowed at the unusual sight of an open fire.

After supper Gavotte took a little stroll and returned with a couple of grouse for our breakfast. After dark we sat around the fire eating peanuts and listening to Gavotte and Mrs. Louderer telling stories of their different great forests. But soon Gavotte took his big sleeping-bag and retired to another cabin, warning us that we must be up early. Our improvised beds were the most comfortable things; I love the flicker of an open fire, the smell of the pines, the pure, sweet air, and I went to sleep thinking how blest I was to be able to enjoy the things I love most.

It seemed only a short time until some one knocked on our door and we were all wide awake in a minute. The fire had burned down and only a soft, indistinct glow from the embers lighted the room, while through a hole in the roof I could see a star glimmering frostily. It was Gavotte at the door and he called through a crack saying he had been hearing queer noises for an hour and he was going to investigate. He had called us so that we need not be alarmed should we hear the noise and not find him. We scrambled into our clothes quickly and ran outdoors to listen.

I can never describe to you the weird beauty of a moonlight night among the pines when the snow is sparkling and gleaming, the deep silence unbroken even by the snapping of a twig. We stood shivering and straining our ears and were about to go back to bed when we heard faintly a long-drawn wail as if all the suffering and sorrow on earth were bound up in that one sound. We couldn't tell which way it came from; it seemed to vibrate through the air and chill our hearts. I had heard that panthers cried that way, but Gavotte said it was not a panther. He said the engine and saws had been moved from where we were to another spring across the *cañon* a mile away, where timber for sawing was more plentiful, but he supposed every one had left the mill when the water froze so they couldn't saw. He added that some one must have remained and was, perhaps, in need of help, and if we were not afraid he would leave us and go see what was wrong.

We went in, made up the fire, and sat in silence, wondering what we should see or hear next. Once or twice that agonized cry came shivering through the cold moonlight. After an age, we heard Gavotte crunching through the snow, whistling cheerily to reassure us. He had crossed the *cañon* to the new mill camp, where he had found two women, loggers' wives, and some children. One of the women, he said, was "so ver' seek," 't was she who was wailing so, and it was the kind of "seek" where we could be of every help and comfort.

Mrs. Louderer stayed and took care of the children while Mrs. O'Shaughnessy and I followed after Gavotte, panting and stumbling, through the snow. Gavotte said he suspected they were short of "needfuls," so he had filled his pockets with coffee and sugar, took in a bottle some of the milk I brought for Baby, and his own flask of whiskey, without which he never travels.

At last, after what seemed to me hours of scrambling through the snow, through deepest gloom where pines were thickest, and out again into patches of white moonlight, we reached the ugly clearing where the new camp stood. Gavotte escorted us to the door and then returned to our camp. Entering, we saw the poor, little soon-to-be mother huddled on her poor bed, while an older woman stood near warning her that the oil would soon be all gone and they would be in darkness. She told us that the sick one had been in pain all the day before and much of the night, and that she herself was worn completely out. So Mrs. O'Shaughnessy sent her to bed and we took charge.

Secretly, I felt it all to be a big nuisance to be dragged out from my warm, comfortable bed to traipse through the snow at that time of the night. But the moment poor little Molly spoke I was glad I was living, because she was a poor little Southern girl whose husband is a Mormon. He had been sent on a mission to Alabama, and the poor girl had fallen in love with his handsome face and knew nothing of Mormonism, so she had run away with him. She thought it would be so grand to live in the glorious West with so splendid a man as she believed her husband to be. But now she believed she was going to die and she was glad of it because she could not return to her "folks," and she said she knew her husband was dead because he and the other woman's husband, both of whom had intended to stay there all winter and cut logs, had gone two weeks before to get their summer's wages and buy supplies. Neither man had come back and there was not a horse or any other way to get out of the mountains to hunt them, so they believed the men to be frozen somewhere on the road.

Rather a dismal prospect, wasn't it? Molly was just longing for some little familiar thing, so I was glad I have not yet gotten rid of my Southern way of talking. No Westerner can ever understand a Southerner's need of sympathy, and, however kind their hearts, they are unable to give it. Only a Southerner can understand how dear are our peculiar words and phrases, and poor little Molly took new courage when she found I knew what she meant when she said she was just "honin'" after a friendly voice.

Well, soon we had the water hot and had filled some bottles and placed them around our patient, and after a couple of hours the tiny little stranger came into the world. It had been necessary to have a great fire in order to have light, so as soon as we got Baby dressed I opened the door a little to cool the room and Molly saw the morning star twinkling merrily. "Oh," she said, "that is what I will call my little girlie,—Star, dear little Star."

It is strange, isn't it? how our spirits will revive after some great ordeal. Molly had been sure she was going to die and saw nothing to live for; now that she had had a cup of hot milk and held her red little baby close, she was just as happy and hopeful as if she had never left her best friends and home to follow the uncertain fortunes of young Will Crosby. So she and I talked of ash-hoppers, smoke-houses, cotton-patches, goobers, poke-greens, and shoats, until she fell asleep.

Soon day was abroad, and so we went outdoors for a fresh breath. The other woman came out just then to ask after Molly. She invited us into her cabin, and, oh, the little Mormons were everywhere; poor, half-clad little things! Some sour-dough biscuit and a can of condensed milk was everything they had to eat. The mother explained to us that their "men" had gone to get things for them, but had not come back, so she guessed they had got drunk and were likely in jail. She told it in a very unconcerned manner. Poor thing! Years of such experience had taught her that blessed are they who expect nothing, for they shall not be disappointed. She said that if Molly had not been sick she would have walked down out of the mountains and got help.

Just then two shots rang out in quick succession, and soon Gavotte came staggering along with a deer across his shoulders. That he left for the family. From our camp he had brought some bacon and butter for Molly, and, poor though it may seem, it was a treat for her. Leaving the woman to dress the venison with her oldest boy's aid, we put out across the *cañon* for our own breakfast. Beside our much-beaten trail hung the second venison, and when we reached our camp and had our own delicious breakfast of grouse, bread, butter, and coffee, Gavotte took Chub and went for our venison. In a short time we were rolling homeward. Of course it didn't take us nearly so long to get home because it was downhill and the road was clearly marked, so in a couple of hours we were home.

Gavotte knew the two loggers were in Green River and were then at work storing ice for the railroad, but he had not known that their wives were left as they were. The men actually had got drunk, lost their money, and were then trying to replace it. After we debated a bit we decided we could not enjoy Christmas with those people in want up there in the cold. Then we got busy. It is sixty miles to town, although our nearest point to the railroad is but forty, so you see it was impossible to get to town to get anything. You should have seen us! Every old garment that had ever been left by men who have worked here was hauled out, and Mrs. O'Shaughnessy's deft fingers soon had a pile of garments cut. We kept the machine humming until far into the night, as long as we could keep our eyes open.

All next day we sewed as hard as we could, and Gavotte cooked as hard as he could. We had intended to have a tree for Jerrine, so we had a box of candles and a box of Christmas snow. Gavotte asked for all the bright paper we could find. We had lots of it, and I think you would be surprised at the possibilities of a little waste paper. He made gorgeous birds, butterflies, and flowers out of paper that once wrapped parcels. Then he asked us for some silk thread, but I had none, so he told us to comb our hair and give him the combings. We did, and with a drop of mucilage he would fasten a hair to a bird's back and then hold it up by the hair. At a few feet's distance it looked exactly as though the bird was flying.

I was glad I had a big stone jar full of *fondant*, because we had a lot of fun shaping and colouring candies. We offered a prize for the best representation of a "nigger," and we had two dozen chocolate-covered things that might have been anything from a monkey to a mouse. Mrs. Louderer cut up her big plum pudding and put it into a dozen small bags. These Gavotte carefully covered with green paper. Then we tore up the holly wreath that Aunt Mary sent me, and put a sprig in the top of each green bag of pudding. I never had so much fun in my life as I had preparing for that Christmas.

At ten o'clock, the morning of the 24th, we were again on our way up the mountain-side. We took shovels so we could clear a road if need be. We had dinner at the old camp, and then Gavotte hunted us a way out to the new, and we smuggled our things into Molly's cabin so the children should have a real surprise. Poor, hopeless little things! Theirs was, indeed, a dull outlook.

Gavotte busied himself in preparing one of the empty cabins for us and in making the horses comfortable. He cut some pine boughs to do that with, and so they paid no attention when he cut a small tree. In the meantime we had cleared everything from Molly's cabin but her bed; we wanted her to see the fun. The children were sent to the spring to water the horses and they were all allowed to ride, so that took them out of the way while Gavotte nailed the tree into a box he had filled with dirt to hold it steady.

There were four women of us, and Gavotte, so it was only the work of a few moments to get the tree ready, and it was the most beautiful one I ever saw. Your largest bell, dear Mrs. Coney, dangled from the topmost branch. Gavotte had attached a long, stout wire to your Santa Claus, so he was able to make him dance frantically without seeming to do so. The hairs that held the birds and butterflies could not be seen, and the effect was beautiful. We had a bucket of apples rubbed bright, and these we fastened to the tree just as they grew on their own branches. The puddings looked pretty, too, and we had done up the parcels that held the clothes as attractively as we could. We saved the candy and the peanuts to put in their little stockings.

As soon as it was dark we lighted the candles and then their mother called the children. Oh, if you could have seen them! It was the very first Christmas tree they had ever seen and they didn't know what to do. The very first present Gavotte handed out was a pair of trousers for eight-years-old Brig, but he just stood and stared at the tree until his brother next in size, with an eye to the main chance, got behind him and pushed him forward, all the time exclaiming, "Go on, can't you! They ain't doin' nothin' to you, they's just doin' somethin' for you." Still Brig would not put out his hand. He just shook his tousled sandy head and said he wanted a bird. So the fun kept up for an hour. Santa had for Molly a package of oatmeal, a pound of butter, a Mason jar of cream, and a dozen eggs, so that she could have suitable food to eat until something could be done.

After the presents had all been distributed we put the phonograph on a box and had a dandy concert. We played "There were Shepherds," "*Ave Maria,*" and "Sweet Christmas Bells." Only we older people cared for those, so then we had "Arrah Wanna," "Silver Bells," "Rainbow," "Red Wing," and such songs. How delighted they were! Our concert lasted two hours, and by that time the little fellows were so sleepy that the excitement no longer affected them and they were put to bed, but they hung up their stockings first, and even Molly hung hers up too. We filled them with peanuts and candy, putting the lion's share of "niggers" into Molly's stocking.

Next morning the happiness broke out in new spots. The children were all clean and warm, though I am afraid I can't brag on the fit of all the clothes. But the pride of the wearers did away with the necessity of a fit. The mother was radiantly thankful for a warm petticoat; that it was made of a blanket too small for a bed didn't bother her, and the stripes were around the bottom anyway. Molly openly rejoiced in her new gown, and that it was made of ugly gray outing flannel she didn't know nor care. Baby Star Crosby looked perfectly sweet in her little new clothes, and her little gown had blue sleeves and they thought a white skirt only added to its beauty. And so it was about everything. We all got so much out of so little. I will never again allow even the smallest thing to go to waste. We were every one just as happy as we could be, almost as delighted as Molly was over her "niggers," and there was very little given that had not been thrown away or was not just odds and ends.

There was never anything more true than that it is more blessed to give than to receive. We certainly had a delicious dinner too, and we let Molly have all she wanted that we dared allow her to eat. The roast venison was so good that we were tempted to let her taste it, but we thought better of that. As soon as dinner was over we packed our belongings and betook ourselves homeward.

It was just dusk when we reached home. Away off on a bare hill a wolf barked. A big owl hooted lonesomely among the pines, and soon a pack of yelping coyotes went scampering across the frozen waste.

It was not the Christmas I had in mind when I sent the card, but it was a *dandy* one, just the same.

With best wishes for you for a happy, *happy* New Year,

Sincerely your friend,

Elinore Rupert Stewart.

20

The Joys of Homesteading

January 23, 1913.

Dear Mrs. Coney,—

I am afraid all my friends think I am very forgetful and that you think I am ungrateful as well, but I am going to plead not guilty. Right after Christmas Mr. Stewart came down with *la grippe* and was so miserable that it kept me busy trying to relieve him. Out here where we can get no physician we have to dope ourselves, so that I had to be housekeeper, nurse, doctor, and general overseer. That explains my long silence.

And now I want to thank you for your kind thought in prolonging our Christmas. The magazines were much appreciated. They relieved some weary night-watches, and the box did Jerrine more good than the medicine I was having to give her for *la grippe*. She was content to stay in bed and enjoy the contents of her box.

When I read of the hard times among the Denver poor, I feel like urging them every one to get out and file on land. I am very enthusiastic about women homesteading. It really requires less strength and labour to raise plenty to satisfy a large family than it does to go out to wash, with the added satisfaction of knowing that their job will not be lost to them if they care to keep it. Even if improving the place does go slowly, it is that much done to stay done. Whatever is raised is the homesteader's own, and there is no house-rent to pay. This year Jerrine cut and dropped enough potatoes to raise a ton of fine potatoes. She wanted to try, so we let her, and you will remember that she is but six years old. We had a man to break the ground and cover the potatoes for her and the man irrigated them once. That was all that was done until digging time, when they were ploughed out and Jerrine picked them up. Any woman strong enough to go out by the day could have done every bit of the work and put in two or three times that much, and it would have been so much more pleasant than to work so hard in the city and then be on starvation rations in the winter.

To me, homesteading is the solution of all poverty's problems, but I realise that temperament has much to do with success in any undertaking, and persons afraid of coyotes and work and loneliness had better let ranching alone. At the same time, any woman who can stand her own company, can see the beauty of the sunset, loves growing things, and is willing to put in as much time at careful labour as she does over the washtub, will certainly succeed; will have independence, plenty to eat all the time, and a home of her own in the end.

Experimenting need cost the homesteader no more than the work, because by applying to the Department of Agriculture at Washington he can get enough of any seed and as many kinds as he wants to make a thorough trial, and it doesn't even cost postage. Also one can always get bulletins from there and from the Experiment Station of one's own State concerning any problem or as many problems as may come up. I would not, for anything, allow Mr. Stewart to do anything toward improving my place, for I want the fun and the experience myself. And I want to be able to speak from experience when I tell others what they can do. Theories are very beautiful, but facts are what must be had, and what I intend to give some time.

Here I am boring you to death with things that cannot interest you! You'd think I wanted you to homestead, wouldn't you? But I am only thinking of the troops of tired, worried women, sometimes even cold and hungry, scared to death of losing their places to work, who could have plenty to eat, who could have good fires by gathering the wood, and comfortable homes of their own, if they but had the courage and determination to get them.

I must stop right now before you get so tired you will not answer. With much love to you from Jerrine and myself, I am

Yours affectionately,

Elinore Rupert Stewart.

21

A Letter of Jerrine's

February 26, 1913.

Dear Mrs. Coney,—

I think you will excuse my mama for not writing to thank you for black Beauty when I tell you why. I wanted to thank you myself, and I wanted to hear it read first so I could very trully thank. Mama always said horses do not talk, but now she knows they do since she read the Dear little book. I have known it along time. My own pony told me the story is very true. Many times I have see men treat horses very badly, but our Clyde dont, and wont let a workman stay if He hurts stock. I am very glad.

Mr Edding came past one day with a load of hay. he had too much load to pull up hill and there was much ice and snow but he think he can make them go up so he fighted and sweared but they could not get up. Mama tried to lend him some horse to help but he was angry and was termined to make his own pull it but at last he had to take off some hay I wish he may read my *Black Beauty*.

Our Clyde is still away. We were going to visit Stella. Mama was driving, the horses raned away. We goed very fast as the wind. I almost fall out Mama hanged on to the lines. if she let go we may all be kill. At last she raned them into a fence. they stop and a man ran to help so we are well but mama hands and arms are still so sore she cant write you yet. My brother Calvin is very sweet. God had to give him to us because he squealed so much he sturbed the angels. We are not angels so he Dont sturb us. I thank you for my good little book. and I love you for it too.

very speakfully,

Jerrine Rupert.

22

The Efficient Mrs. O'shaughnessy

May 5, 1913.

Dear Mrs. Coney,—

Your letter of April 25 certainly was a surprise, but a very welcome one. We are so rushed with spring work that we don't even go to the office for the mail, and I owe you letters and thanks. I keep promising myself the pleasure of writing you and keep putting it off until I can have more leisure, but that time never gets here. I am so glad when I can bring a little of this big, clean, beautiful outdoors into your apartment for you to enjoy, and I can think of nothing that would give me more happiness than to bring the West and its people to others who could not otherwise enjoy them. If I could only take them from whatever is worrying them and give them this bracing mountain air, glimpses of the scenery, a smell of the pines and the sage,—if I could only make them feel the free, ready sympathy and hospitality of these frontier people, I am sure their worries would diminish and my happiness would be complete.

Little Star Crosby is growing to be the sweetest little kid. Her mother tells me that she is going "back yan" when she gets a "little mo' richer." I am afraid you give me too much credit for being of help to poor little Molly. It wasn't that I am so helpful, but that "fools rush in where angels fear to tread." It was Mrs. O'Shaughnessy who was the real help. She is a woman of great courage and decision and of splendid sense and judgment. A few days ago a man she had working for her got his finger-nail mashed off and neglected to care for it. Mrs. O'Shaughnessy examined it and found that gangrene had set in. She didn't tell him, but made various preparations and then told him she had heard that if there was danger of blood-poisoning it would show if the finger was placed on wood and the patient looked toward the sun. She said the person who looked at the finger could then see if there was any poison. So the man placed his finger on the chopping-block and before he could bat his eye she had chopped off the black, swollen finger. It was so sudden and unexpected that there seemed to be no pain.

Then Mrs. O'Shaughnessy showed him the green streak already starting up his arm. The man seemed dazed and she was afraid of shock, so she gave him a dose of morphine and whiskey. Then with a quick stroke of a razor she laid open the green streak and immersed the whole arm in a strong solution of bichloride of mercury for twenty minutes. She then dressed the wound with absorbent cotton saturated with olive oil and carbolic acid, bundled her patient into a buggy, and drove forty-five miles that night to get him to a doctor. The doctor told us that only her quick action and knowledge of what to do saved the man's life.

I was surprised that you have had a letter from Jerrine. I knew she was writing to you that day, but I was feeling very stiff and sore from the runaway and had lain down. She kept asking me how to spell words until I told her I was too tired and wanted to sleep. While I was asleep the man came for the mail, so she sent her letter. I have your address on the back of the writing-pad, so she knew she had it right, but I suspect that was all she had right. She has written you many let-ters but I have never allowed her to send them because she misspells, but that time she stole a march on me. The books you sent her, "Black Beauty" and "Alice in Wonderland," have given her more pleasure than anything she has ever had. She just loves them and is saving them, she says, for her own little girls. She is very confident that the stork will one day visit her and leave her a "very many" little girls. They are to be of assorted sizes. She says she can't see why I order all my babies little and red and squally,—says she thinks God had just as soon let me have larger ones, especially as I get so many from him.

One day before long I will get busy and write you of a visit I shall make to a Mormon bishop's household. Polygamy is still practiced.

Very truly your friend,

Elinore Rupert Stewart.

23

How it Happened

June 12, 1913.

Dear Mrs. Coney,—

Your letter of the 8th to hand, and in order to catch you before you leave I'll answer at once and not wait for time. I always think I shall do better with more time, but with three "bairns," garden, chickens, cows, and housework I don't seem to find much time for anything. Now for the first question. My maiden name was Pruitt, so when I am putting on airs I sign Elinore Pruitt Stewart. I don't think I have ever written anything that Clyde would object to, so he can still stay on the pedestal Scotch custom puts him upon and remain "the Stewart." Indeed, I don't think you are too inquisitive, and I am glad to tell you how I happened to meet the "gude mon."

It all happened because I had a stitch in my side. When I was housekeeper at the Nursery, I also had to attend to the furnace, and, strange but true, the furnace was built across the large basement from where the coal was thrown in, so I had to tote the coal over, and my *modus operandi* was to fill a tub with coal and then drag it across to the hungry furnace. Well, one day I felt the catch and got no better fast. After Dr. F—— punched and prodded, she said, "Why, you have the *grippe*." Rev. Father Corrigan had been preparing me to take the Civil-Service examination, and that afternoon a lesson was due, so I went over to let him see how little I knew. I was in pain and was so blue that I could hardly speak without weeping, so I told the Reverend Father how tired I was of the rattle and bang, of the glare and the soot, the smells and the hurry. I told him what I longed for was the sweet, free open, and that I would like to homestead. That was Saturday evening. He advised me to go straight uptown and put an "ad" in the paper, so as to get it into the Sunday paper. I did so, and because I wanted as

110

much rest and quiet as possible I took Jerrine and went uptown and got a nice quiet room.

On the following Wednesday I received a letter from Clyde, who was in Boulder visiting his mother. He was leaving for Wyoming the following Saturday and wanted an interview, if his proposition suited me. I was so glad of his offer, but at the same time I couldn't know what kind of person he was; so, to lessen any risk, I asked him to come to the Sunshine Mission, where Miss Ryan was going to help me "size him up." He didn't know that part of it, of course, but he stood inspection admirably. I was under the impression he had a son, but he hadn't, and he and his mother were the very last of their race. I am as proud and happy today as I was the day I became his wife. I wish you knew him, but I suspect I had better not brag too much, lest you think me not quite sincere. He expected to visit you while he was in Boulder. He went to the Stock Show, but was with a party, so he planned to go again. But before he could, the man he left here, and whom I dismissed for drunkenness, went to Boulder and told him I was alone, so the foolish thing hurried home to keep me from too hard work. So that is why he was disappointed.

Junior can talk quite well, and even Calvin jabbers. The children are all well, and Jerrine writes a little every day to you. I have been preparing a set of indoor outings for invalids. Your telling me your invalid friends enjoyed the letters suggested the idea. I thought to write of little outings I take might amuse them, but wanted to write just as I took the little trips, while the impressions were fresh; that is why I have not sent them before now. Is it too late? Shall I send them to you? Now this is really not a letter; it is just a reply. I must say good-night; it is twelve o'clock, and I am so sleepy.

I do hope you will have a very happy summer, and that you will share your happiness with me in occasional letters.

With much love,

Elinore Stewart.

In writing I forgot to say that the Reverend Father thought it a good plan to get a position as housekeeper for some rancher who would advise me about land and water rights. By keeping house, he pointed out, I could have a home and a living and at the same time see what kind of a homestead I could get.

24

A Little Romance

October 8, 1913.

My dear Friend,—

I have had such a happy little peep into another's romance that I think I should be cheating you if I didn't tell you. Help in this country is extremely hard to get; so when I received a letter from one Aurelia Timmons, saying she wanted a job,—three dollars a week and *not* to be called "Relie,"—my joy could hardly be described. I could hardly wait until morning to start for Bridger Bench, where Aurelia held forth. I was up before the lark next morning. It is more miles to the Bridger Bench country than the "gude mon" wants his horses driven in a day; so permission was only given after I promised to curb my impatience and stay overnight with Mrs. Louderer. Under ordinary circumstances that would have been a pleasure, but I knew at least a dozen women who would any of them seize on to Aurelia and wrest her from me, so it was only after it seemed I would not get to go at all that I promised.

At length the wagon was greased, some oats put in, a substantial lunch and the kiddies loaded in, and I started on my way. Perhaps it was the prospect of getting help that gilded everything with a new beauty. The great mountains were so majestic, and the day so young that I knew the night wind was still murmuring among the pines far up on the mountain-sides. The larks were trying to outdo each other and the robins were so saucy that I could almost have flicked them with the willow I was using as a whip. The rabbit-bush made golden patches everywhere, while purple asters and great pink thistles lent their charm. Going in that direction, our way lay between a mountain stream and the foothills. There are many ranches along the stream, and as we were out so early, we could see the blue smoke curling from each house we passed.

We knew that venison steak, hot biscuit, and odorous coffee would soon grace their tables. We had not had the venison, for the "gude mon" holds to the letter of the law which protects deer here, but we begrudged no one anything; we were having exactly what we wanted. We jogged along happily, if slowly, for I must explain to you that Chub is quite the laziest horse in the State, and Bill, his partner, is so old he stands like a bulldog. He is splay-footed and sway-backed, but he is a beloved member of our family, so I vented my spite on Chub, and the willow descended periodically across his black back, I guess as much from force of habit as anything else. But his hide is thick and his memory short, so we broke no record that day.

We drove on through the fresh beauty of the morning, and when the sun was straight overhead we came to the last good water we could expect before we reached Mrs. Louderer's; so we stopped for lunch. In Wyoming quantity has a great deal more to do with satisfaction than does quality; after half a day's drive you won't care so much what it is you're going to eat as you will that there is enough of it. That is a lesson I learned long ago; so our picnic was real. There were no ants in the pie, but that is accounted for by there being no pie. Our road had crossed the creek, and we were resting in the shade of a quaking-asp grove, high up on the sides of the Bad Land hills. For miles far below lay the valley through which we had come.

Farther on, the mountains with their dense forests were all wrapped in the blue haze of the melancholy days. Soon we quitted our enchanted grove whose quivering, golden leaves kept whispering secrets to us.

About three o'clock we came down out of the hills on to the bench on which the Louderer ranch is situated. Perhaps I should explain that this country is a series of huge terraces, each terrace called a bench. I had just turned into the lane that leads to the house when a horseman came cantering toward me. "Hello!" he saluted, as he drew up beside the wagon. "Goin' up to the house? Better not. Mrs. Louderer is not at home, and there's no one there but Greasy Pete. He's on a tear; been drunk two days, I'm tellin' you. He's *full* of mischief. 'T ain't safe around old Greasy. I advise you to go some'eres else."

"Well," I asked, "where *can* I go?"

"Danged if I know," he replied, "'lessen it 's to Kate Higbee's. She lives about six or seven miles west. She ain't been here long, but I guess you can't miss her place. Just jog along due west till you get to

Red Gulch ravine, then turn north for a couple of miles. You'll see her cabin up against a cedar ridge. Well, so 'long!" He dug his spurs into his cayuse's side and rode on.

Tears of vexation so blinded me that I could scarcely see to turn the team, but ominous sounds and wild yells kept coming from the house, so I made what haste I could to get away from such an unpleasant neighbourhood. Soon my spirits began to rise. Kate Higbee, I reflected, was likely to prove to be an interesting person. All Westerners are likable, with the possible exception of Greasy Pete. I rather looked forward to my visit. But my guide had failed to mention the buttes; so, although I jogged as west as I knew how, I found I had to wind around a butte about ever so often. I crossed a ravine with equal frequency, and all looked alike. It is not surprising that soon I could not guess where I was. We could turn back and retrace our tracks, but actual danger lay there; so it seemed wiser to push on, as there was, perhaps, no greater danger than discomfort ahead.

The sun hung like a big red ball ready to drop into the hazy distance when we came clear of the buttes and down on to a broad plateau, on which grass grew plentifully. That encouraged me because the horses need not suffer, and if I could make the scanty remnant of our lunch do for the children's supper and breakfast, we could camp in comfort, for we had blankets. But we must find water. I stood up in the wagon and, shading my eyes against the sun's level light, was looking out in the most promising directions when I noticed that the plateau's farther side was bounded by a cedar ridge, and, better yet, a smoke was slowly rising, column-like, against the dun prospect. That, I reasoned, must be my destination. Even the horses livened their paces, and in a little while we were there.

But no house greeted our eyes,—just a big camp-fire. A lean old man sat on a log-end and surveyed us indifferently. On the ground lay a large canvas-covered pack, apparently unopened. An old saddle lay up against a cedar-trunk. Two old horses grazed near. I was powerfully disappointed. You know misery loves company; so I ventured to say, "Good-evening."

He didn't stir, but he grunted, "Hello."

I knew then that he was not a fossil, and hope began to stir in my heart. Soon he asked, "Are you goin' somewheres or jist travelin'?"

I told him I had started somewhere, but reckoned I must be travelling, as I had not gotten there. Then he said, "My name is Hiram K. Hull. Whose woman are you?" I confessed to belonging to the house of Stewart.

"Which Stewart?" he persisted,—"C.R., S.W., or H.C.?" Again I owned up truthfully. "Well," he continued, "what does he mean by letting you gad about in such onconsequential style?"

Sometimes a woman gets too angry to talk. Don't you believe that? No? Well, they do, I assure you, for I was then. He seemed grown to the log. As he had made no move to help me, without answering him I clambered out of the wagon and began to take the horses loose. "Ho!" he said; "are you goin' to camp here?"

"Yes, I am," I snapped. "Have you any objections?"

"Oh, no, none that won't keep," he assured me. It has always been a theory of mine that when we become sorry for ourselves we make our misfortunes harder to bear, because we lose courage and can't think without bias; so I cast about me for something to be glad about, and the comfort that at least we were safer with a simpleton than near a drunken Mexican came to me; so I began to view the situation with a little more tolerance.

After attending to the horses I began to make the children comfortable. My unwilling host sat silently on his log, drawing long and hard at his stubby old pipe. How very little there was left of our lunch! Just for meanness I asked him to share with us, and, if you'll believe me, he did. He gravely ate bread-rims and scraps of meat until there was not one bit left for even the baby's breakfast. Then he drew the back of his hand across his mouth and remarked, "I should think when you go off on a ja'nt like this you'd have a well-filled mess-box." Again speech failed me.

Among some dwarf willows not far away a spring bubbled. I took the kiddies there to prepare them for rest. When I returned to the fire, what a transformation! The pack was unrolled and blankets were spread, the fire had been drawn aside, disclosing a bean-hole, out of which Hiram K. was lifting an oven. He took off the lid. Two of the plumpest, brownest ducks that ever tempted any one were fairly swimming in gravy. Two loaves of what he called punk, with a box of crackers, lay on a newspaper. He mimicked me exactly when he asked me to take supper with him, and I tried hard to imitate him in promptitude when I accepted. The babies had some of the crackers wet with hot water and a little of the gravy. We soon had the rest looking scarce. The big white stars were beginning to twinkle before we were through, but the camp-fire was bright, and we all felt better-natured. Men are not alone in having a way to their heart through their stomach.

I made our bed beneath the wagon, and Hiram K. fixed his canvas around, so we should be sheltered. I felt so much better and thought so much better of him that I could laugh and chat gayly. "Now, tell me," he asked, as he fastened the canvas to a wheel, "didn't you think I was an old devil at first?"

"Yes, I did," I answered.

"Well," he said, "I am; so you guessed right."

After I put the children to bed, we sat by the fire and talked awhile. I told him how I happened to be gadding about in "such onconse-quential" style, and he told me stories of when the country was new and fit to live in. "Why," he said, in a burst of enthusiasm, "time was once when you went to bed you were not sure whether you'd get up alive and with your scalp on or not, the Injins were that thick. And then there was white men a durned sight worse; they were likely to plug you full of lead just to see you kick. But now," he continued mournfully, "a bear or an antelope, maybe an elk, is about all the excitement we can expect. Them good old days are gone." I am mighty glad of it; a drunken Pete is bad enough for me.

I was tired, so soon I went to bed. I could hear him as he cut cedar boughs for his own fireside bed, and as he rattled around among his pots and pans. Did you ever eat pork and beans heated in a frying-pan on a camp-fire for breakfast? Then if you have not, there is one delight left you. But you must be away out in Wyoming, with the morning sun just gilding the distant peaks, and your pork and beans must be out of a can, heated in a disreputable old frying-pan, served with cof-fee *boiled* in a battered old pail and drunk from a tomato-can. You'll *never* want iced melons, powdered sugar, and fruit, or sixty-nine varie-ties of breakfast food, if once you sit Trilby-wise on Wyoming sand and eat the kind of breakfast we had that day.

After breakfast Hiram K. Hull hitched our horses to the wagon, got his own horses ready, and then said, "'T ain't more 'n half a mile straight out between them two hills to the stage-road, but I guess I had better go and show you exactly, or you will be millin' around here all day, tryin' to find it." In a very few minutes we were on the road, and our odd host turned to go. "S'long!" he called. "Tell Stewart you seen old Hikum. Him and me's shared tarps many's the nights. We used to be punchers together,—old Clyde and me. Tell him old Hikum ain't forgot him." So saying, he rode away into the golden morning, and we drove onward, too.

We stopped for lunch only a few minutes that day, and we reached the Bridger community about two that afternoon. The much sought Aurelia had accepted the position of lifetime housekeeper for a sheep-herder who had no house to keep, so I had to cast about for whatever comfort I could.

The roadhouse is presided over by a very able body of the clan of Ferguson. I had never met her, but formalities count for very little in the West. She was in her kitchen, having more trouble, she said, than a hen whose ducklings were in swimming. I asked her if she could ac-commodate the children and myself. "Yes," she said, "I can give you a bed and grub, but I ain't got no time to ask you nothing. I ain't got no time to inquire who you are nor where you come from. There's one room left. You can have that, but you'll have to look out for yourself and young 'uns." I felt equal to that; so I went out to have the horses cared for and to unload the kiddies.

Leaning against the wagon was a man who made annual rounds of all the homes in our community each summer; his sole object was to see what kind of flowers we succeeded with. Every woman in our neighbourhood knows Bishey Bennet, but I don't think many would have recognized him that afternoon. I had never seen him dressed in anything but blue denim overalls and overshirt to match, but today he proudly displayed what he said was his dove-coloured suit. The style must have been one of years ago, for I cannot remember seeing trou-sers quite so skimpy. He wore top-boots, but as a concession to fashion he wore the boot-tops under the trouser-legs, and as the trousers were about as narrow as a sheath skirt, they kept slipping up and gave the appearance of being at least six inches too short. Although Bishey is tall and thin, his coat was two sizes too small, his shirt was of soft tan material, and he wore a blue tie. But whatever may have been amiss with his costume was easily forgotten when one saw his radiant face. He grasped my hand and wrung it as if it was a chicken's neck.

"What in the world is the matter with you?" I asked, as I rubbed my abused paw. "Just you come here and I'll tell you," he answered. There was no one to hear but the kiddies, but I went around the corner of the house with him. He put his hand up to his mouth and whispered that "Miss Em'ly" was coming, would be there on the af-ternoon stage. I had never heard of "Miss Em'ly," and said so. "Well, just you go in and set on the sofy and soon's I see your horses took care of I'll come in and tell you." I went into my own room, and af-ter I rustled some water I made myself and the kiddies a little more presentable. Then we went into the sitting-room and sat on the "sofy."

Presently Bishey sauntered in, trying to look unconcerned and at ease, but he was so fidgety he couldn't sit down. But he told his story, and a dear one it is.

It seems that back in New York State he and Miss Em'ly were "young uns" together. When they were older they planned to marry, but neither wanted to settle down to the humdrumness that they had always known. Both dreamed of the golden West; so Bishey had gone to blaze the trail, and "Miss Em'ly" was to follow. First one duty and then another had held her, until twenty-five years had slipped by and they had not seen each other, but now she was coming, that very day. They would be married that evening, and I at once appointed myself matron of honour and was plumb glad there was no other candidate.

I at once took the decorations in hand. Bishey, Jerrine, and myself went out and gathered armfuls of asters and goldenrod-like rabbit-brush. From the dump-pile we sorted cans and pails that would hold water, and we made the sitting-room a perfect bower of purple and gold beauty. I put on my last clean shirt-waist and the children's last clean dresses. Then, as there seemed nothing more to do, Bishey suggested that we walk up the road and meet the stage; but the day had been warm, and I remembered my own appearance when I had come over that same road the first time. I knew that journey was trying on any one's appearance at any time of the year, and after twenty-five years to be thrust into view covered with alkali dust and with one's hat on awry would be too much for feminine patience; so I pointed out to Bishey that he'd better clear out and let Miss Em'ly rest a bit before he showed up. At last he reluctantly agreed.

I went out to the kitchen to find what could be expected in the way of hot water for Miss Em'ly when she should come. I found I could have all I wanted if I heated it myself. Mrs. Ferguson could not be bothered about it, because a water company had met there to vote on new canals, the sheep-men were holding a convention, there was a more than usual run of transients besides the regular boarders, and supper was ordered for the whole push. All the help she had was a girl she just knew didn't have sense enough to pound sand into a rat-hole. Under those circumstances I was mighty glad to help. I put water on to heat and then forgot Miss Em'ly, I was enjoying helping so much, until I heard a door slam and saw the stage drive away toward the barn.

I hastened to the room I knew was reserved for Miss Em'ly. I rapped on the door, but it was only opened a tiny crack. I whispered through that I was a neighbour-friend of Mr. Bennet's, that I had lots of hot water for her and had come to help her if I might. Then she opened the door, and I entered. I found a very travel-stained little woman, down whose dust-covered cheeks tears had left their sign. Her prettiness was the kind that wins at once and keeps you ever after. She was a strange mixture of stiff reticence and childish trust. She was in *such* a flutter, and she said she was ashamed to own it, but she was so hungry she could hardly wait.

After helping her all I could, I ran out to see about the wedding supper that was to be served before the wedding. I found that no special supper had been prepared. It seemed to me a shame to thrust them down among the water company, the convention, the regulars, and the transients, and I mentally invited myself to the wedding supper and began to plan how we could have a little privacy. The carpenters were at work on a long room off the kitchen that was to be used as storeroom and pantry. They had gone for the day, and their saw-horses and benches were still in the room. It was only the work of a moment to sweep the sawdust away. There was only one window, but it was large and in the west. It took a little time to wash that, but it paid to do it. When a few asters and sprays of rabbit-brush were placed in a broken jar on the window-sill, there was a picture worth seeing. Some planks were laid on the saw-horses, some papers over them, and a clean white cloth over all. I sorted the dishes myself; the prettiest the house afforded graced our table. I rubbed the glassware until it shone almost as bright as Bishey's smile.

Bishey had come when he could stay away no longer; he and Miss Em'ly had had their first little talk, so they came out to where I was laying the table. They were both beaming. Miss Em'ly took hold at once to help. "Bishey," she commanded, "do you go at once to where my boxes are open, the one marked 7; bring me a blue jar you'll find in one corner." He went to do her bidding, and I to see about the kiddies. When I came back with them, there was a small willow basket in the center of our improvised table, heaped high with pears, apples, and grapes all a little the worse for their long journey from New York State to Wyoming, but still things of beauty and a joy as long as they lasted to Wyoming eyes and appetites.

We had a perfectly roasted leg of lamb; we had mint sauce, a pyramid of flaky mashed potatoes, a big dish of new peas, a plate of sponge-cake I will be long in forgetting; and the blue jar was full of grape marmalade. Our iced tea was exactly right; the pieces of ice clinked pleasantly against our glasses. We took our time, and we were all happy. We could all see the beautiful sunset, its last rays lingering on Miss Em'ly's abundant auburn hair to make happy the bride the sun shines on. We saw the wonderful colours—orange, rose, and violet—creep up and fade into darker shades, until at last mellow dusk filled the room. Then I took the kiddies to my room to be put to bed while I should wait until time for the ceremony.

Soon the babies were sleeping, and Jerrine and I went into the sitting-room. They were sitting on the "sofy." She was telling him that the apples had come from the tree they had played under, the pears from the tree they had set out, the grapes from the vine over the well. She told him of things packed in her boxes, everything a part of the past they both knew. He in turn told her of his struggles, his successes, and some of what he called his failures. She was a most encouraging little person, and she'd say to him, "You did well, Bishey. I'll say *that* for you: you did well!" Then he told her about the flowers he had planted for her. I understood then why he acted so queerly about my flowers. It happens that I am partial to old-time favourites, and I grow as many of them as I can get to succeed in this altitude; so I have zinnias, marigolds, hollyhocks, and many other dear old flowers that my mother loved. Many of them had been the favourites of Miss Em'ly's childhood, but Bishey hadn't remembered the names; so he had visited us all, and when he found a flower he remembered, he asked the name and how we grew it, then he tried it, until at last he had about all. Miss Em'ly wiped the tears from her eyes as she remarked, "Bishey, you did well; yes, you did *real* well." I thought to myself how well we could *all* do if we were so encouraged.

At last the white-haired old justice of the peace came, and said the words that made Emily Wheeler the wife of Abisha Bennet. A powerfully noisy but truly friendly crowd wished them well. One polite fellow asked her where she was from. She told him from New York State. "Why," he asked, "do New Yorkers always say *State*?"

"Why, because," she answered,—and her eyes were big with surprise,—"*no* one would want to say they were from New York City."

It had been a trying day for us, so soon Jerrine and I slipped out to our room. Ours was the first room off the sitting-room, and a long hallway led past our door; a bench sat against the wall, and it seemed a favourite roosting-place for people with long discussions. First some fellows were discussing the wedding. One thought Bishey "cracked" because he had shipped out an old cooking-stove, one of the first manufactured, all the way from where he came from, instead of buying a new one nearer home. They recalled instance after instance in which he had acted queerly, but to me his behaviour was no longer a mystery. I know the stove belonged somewhere in the past and that his every act connected past and future.

After they had talked themselves tired, two old fellows took possession of the bench and added a long discussion on how to grow corn to the general din. Even sweet corn cannot be successfully grown at this altitude, yet those old men argued pro and con till I know their throats must have ached. In the sitting-room they all talked at once of ditches, water-contracts, and sheep. I was *so* sleepy. I heard a tired clock away off somewhere strike two. Some sheep-men had the bench and were discussing the relative values of different dips. I reckon my ego must have gotten tangled with some one's else about then, for I found myself sitting up in bed foolishly saying,—

Two old herders, unshaved and hairy,
Whose old tongues are never weary,
Just outside my chamber-door
Prate of sheep dips for ever more.

Next morning it was Bishey's cheerful voice that started my day. I had hoped to be up in time to see them off, but I wasn't. I heard him call out to Mrs. Bishey, "Miss Em'ly, I've got the boxes all loaded. We can start *home* in ten minutes."

I heard her clear voice reply, "You've done well, Bishey. I'll be ready by then."

I was hurriedly dressing, hoping yet to see her, when I heard Bishey call out to bluff old Colonel Winters, who had arrived in the night and had not known of the wedding, "Hello! Winters, have you met Miss Em'ly? Come over here and meet her. I'm a married man now. I married Miss Em'ly last night."

The colonel couldn't have known how apt was his reply when he said, "I'm glad for you, Bishey. You've done well."

I peeked between the curtains, and saw Bishey's wagon piled high with boxes, with Miss Em'ly, self-possessed and happy, greeting the colonel. Soon I heard the rattle of wheels, and the dear old happy pair were on their way to the cabin home they had waited twenty-five years for. Bless the kind old hearts of them! I'm sure they've both "done well."

25

Among the Mormons

November, 1913.

My dear Friend,—

I have wanted to write you for a long time, but have been so busy. I have had some visitors and have been on a visit; I think you would like to hear about it all, so I will tell you.

I don't think you would have admired my appearance the morning this adventure began: I was in the midst of fall house-cleaning which included some papering. I am no expert at the very best, and papering a wall has difficulties peculiar to itself. I was up on a barrel trying to get a long, sloppy strip of paper to stick to the ceiling instead of to me, when in my visitors trooped, and so surprised me that I stepped off the barrel and into a candy-bucket of paste. At the same time the paper came off the ceiling and fell over mine and Mrs. Louderer's head. It was right aggravating, I can tell you, but my visitors were Mrs. O'Shaughnessy and Mrs. Louderer, and no one could stay discouraged with that pair around.

After we had scraped as much paste as we could off ourselves they explained that they had come to take me somewhere. That sounded good to me, but I could not see how I could get off. However, Mrs. Louderer said she had come to keep house and to take care of the children while I should go with Mrs. O'Shaughnessy to E——. We should have two days' travel by sled and a few hours on a train, then another journey by sled. I wanted to go powerfully, but the paste-smeared room seemed to forbid.

As Mrs. Louderer would stay with the children, Mr. Stewart thought the trip would be good for me. Mrs. O'Shaughnessy knew I wanted to visit Bishop D——, a shining light among the Latter-Day Saints, so she promised we should stay overnight at his house. That settled it; so in the cold, blue light of the early morning, Mr. Beeler, a new neighbour, had driven my friends over in Mrs. Louderer's big sled, to which was hitched a pair of her great horses and his own team. He is a widower and was going out to the road for supplies, so it seemed a splendid time to make my long-planned visit to the bishop. Deep snow came earlier this year than usual, and the sledding and weather both promised to be good. It was with many happy anticipations that I snuggled down among the blankets and bearskins that morning.

Mr. Beeler is pleasant company, and Mrs. O'Shaughnessy is so jolly and bright, and I could leave home without a single misgiving with Mrs. Louderer in charge.

The evening sky was blazing crimson and gold, and the mountains behind us were growing purple when we entered the little settlement where the bishop lives. We drove briskly through the scattered, straggling little village, past the store and the meeting-house, and drew up before the dwelling of the bishop. The houses of the village were for the most part small cabins of two or three rooms, but the bishop's was more pretentious. It was a frame building and boasted paint and shutters. A tithing-office stood near, and back of the house we could see a large granary and long stacks of hay. A bunch of cattle was destroying one stack, and Mrs. O'Shaughnessy remarked that the tallow from those cattle should be used when the olive oil gave out at their anointings, because it was the bishop's cattle eating consecrated hay.

We knocked on the door, but got no answer. Mr. Beeler went around to the back, but no one answered, so we concluded we would have to try elsewhere for shelter. Mrs. O'Shaughnessy comforted me by remarking, "Well, there ain't a penny's worth of difference in a Mormon bishop and any other Mormon, and D—— is not the only polygamist by a long shot."

We had just turned out of the gate when a lanky, tow-headed boy about fourteen years of age rode up. We explained our presence there, and the boy explained to us that the bishop and Aunt Debbie were away. The next best house up the road was his "Maw's," he said; so, as Mr. Beeler expected to stay with a friend of his, Mrs. O'Shaughnessy and I determined to see if "Maw" could accommodate us for the night.

Mr. Beeler offered to help the boy get the cattle out, but he said, "No, Paw said it would not matter if they got into the hay, but that he had to knock off some poles on another part of the stockyard so that some horses could get in to eat."

123

Mrs Louderer and Mrs O'Shaughnessy

"But," I asked, "isn't that consecrated hay?—isn't it tithing?"

"Yes," he said, "but that won't hurt a bit, only that old John Ladd always pays his tithe with foxtail hay and it almost ruins Paw's horses' mouths."

I asked him if his father's stock was supposed to get the hay.

"No, I guess not," he said, "but they are always getting in accidental like."

We left him to fix the fence so the horses could get in "accidental like," and drove the short distance to "the next best house."

We were met at the door by a pleasant-faced little woman who hurried us to the fire. We told her our plight. "Why, certainly you must stay with me," she said. "I am glad the bishop and Deb are away. They keep all the company, and I so seldom have anyone come; you see Debbie has no children and can do so much better for any one stopping there than I can, but I like company, too, and I am glad of a chance to keep you. You two can have Maudie's bed. Maud is my oldest girl and she has gone to Ogden to visit, so we have plenty of room."

By now it was quite dark. She lighted a lamp and bustled about, preparing supper. We sat by the stove and, as Mrs. O'Shaughnessy said, "noticed."

Two little boys were getting in wood for the night. They appeared to be about eight years old; they were twins and were the youngest of the family. Two girls, about ten and twelve years old, were assisting our hostess; then the boy Orson, whom we met at the gate, and Maud, the daughter who was away, made up the family. They seemed a happy, contented family, if one judged by appearance alone. After supper the children gathered around the table to prepare next day's lessons. They were bright little folks, but they mingled a great deal of talk with their studies and some of what they talked was family history.

"Mamma," said Kittie, the largest of the little girls, "if Aunt Deb does buy a new coat and you get her old one, then can I have yours?"

"I don't know," her mother replied; "I should have to make it over if you did take it. Maybe we can have a new one."

"No, we can't have a new one, I know, for Aunt Deb said so, but she is going to give me her brown dress and you her gray one; she said so the day I helped her iron. We'll have those to make over."

For the first time I noticed the discontented lines on our hostess's face, and it suddenly occurred to me that we were in the house of the bishop's second wife. Before I knew I was coming on this journey I

125

thought of a dozen questions I wanted to ask the bishop, but I could never ask that care-worn little woman anything concerning their peculiar belief. However, I was spared the trouble, for soon the children retired and the conversation drifted around to Mormonism and polygamy; and our hostess seemed to want to talk, so I just listened, for Mrs. O'Shaughnessy rather likes to "argufy"; but she had no argument that night, only her questions started our hostess's story.

She had been married to the bishop not long before the manifesto, and he had been married several years then to Debbie. But Debbie had no children, and all the money the bishop had to start with had been his first wife's; so when it became necessary for him to discard a wife it was a pretty hard question for him because a little child was coming to the second wife and he had nothing to provide for her with except what his first wife's money paid for. The first wife said she would consent to him starting the second, if she filed on land and paid her back a small sum every year until it was all paid back. So he took the poor "second," after formally renouncing her, and helped her to file on the land she now lives on. He built her a small cabin, and so she started her career as a "second." I suppose the "first" thought she would be rid of the second, who had never really been welcome, although the bishop could never have married a "second" without her consent.

"I would *never* consent," said Mrs. O'Shaughnessy.

"Oh, yes, you would if you had been raised a Mormon," said our hostess. "You see, we were all of us children of polygamous parents. We have been used to plural marriages all our lives. We believe that such experience fits us for our after-life, as we are only preparing for life beyond while here."

"Do you expect to go to heaven, and do you think the man who married you and then discarded you will go to heaven too?" asked Mrs. O'Shaughnessy.

"Of course I do," she replied.

"Then," said Mrs. O'Shaughnessy, "I am afraid if it had been mysilf I'd have been after raising a little hell here intirely."

Our hostess was not offended, and there followed a long recital of earlier-day hard times that you would scarcely believe any one could live through. It seems the first wife in such families is boss, and while they do not live in the same homes, still she can very materially affect the other's comfort.

Mrs. O'Shaughnessy asked her if she had married again.

She said, "No."

"Then," said Mrs. O'Shaughnessy, "whose children are these?"

"My own," she replied.

Mrs. O'Shaughnessy was relentless. "Who is their father?" she asked.

I was right sorry for the poor little woman as she stammered, "I—I don't know."

Then she went on, "Of course I *do* know, and I don't believe you are spying to try to stir up trouble for my husband. Bishop D—— is their father, as he is still my husband, although he had to cast me off to save himself and me. I love him and I see no wrong in him. All the Gentiles have against him is he is a little too smart for them. 'T was their foolish law that made him wrong the children and me, and *not* his wishes."

"But," Mrs. O'Shaughnessy said, "it places your children in such a plight; they can't inherit, they can't even claim his name, they have no status legally."

"Oh, but the bishop will see to that," the little woman answered.

Mrs. O'Shaughnessy asked her if she had still to work as hard as she used to.

"No, I don't believe I do," she said, "for since Mr. D—— has been bishop, things come easier. He built this house with his own money, so Deb has nothing to do with it."

I asked her if she thought she was as happy as "second" as she would be if she was the *only* wife.

"Oh, I don't know," she said, "perhaps not. Deb and me don't always agree. She is jealous of the children and because I am younger, and I get to feeling bad when I think she is perfectly safe as a wife and has no cares. She has everything she wants, and I have to take what I can get, and my children have to wait upon her. But it will all come right somewhere, sometime," she ended cheerfully, as she wiped her eyes with her apron.

I felt so sorry for her and so ashamed to have seen into her sorrow that I was really glad next morning when I heard Mr. Beeler's cheerful voice calling, "All aboard!"

We had just finished breakfast, and few would ever guess that Mrs. D—— knew a trial; she was so cheerful and so cordial as she bade us goodbye and urged us to stop with her every time we passed through.

About noon that day we reached the railroad. The snow had delayed the train farther north, so for once we were glad to have to wait for a train, as it gave us time to get a bite to eat and to wash up a bit. It was not long, however, till we were comfortably seated in the train. I think a train ride might not be so enjoyable to most, but to us it was a delight; I even enjoyed looking at the Negro porter, although I suspect he expected to be called Mister. I found very soon after coming West that I must not say "Uncle" or "Aunty" as I used to at home.

It was not long until they called the name of the town at which we wanted to stop. Mrs. O'Shaughnessy had a few acquaintances there, but we went to a hotel. We were both tired, so as soon as we had supper we went to bed. The house we stopped at was warmer and more comfortable than the average hotel in the West, but the partitions were very thin, so when a couple of "punchers," otherwise cowboys, took the room next to ours, we could hear every word they said.

It appears that one was English and the other a tenderfoot. The tenderfoot was in love with a girl who had filed on a homestead near the ranch on which he was employed, but who was then a waitress in the hotel we were at. She had not seemed kind to the tenderfoot and he was telling his friend about it. The Englishman was trying to instruct him as to how to proceed.

"You need to be *very* circumspect, Johnny, where females are concerned, but you mustn't be too danged timid either."

"I don't know what the devil to say to her; I can barely nod my head when she asks me will I take tea or coffee; and tonight she mixed it because I nodded yes when she said, 'tea or coffee,' and it was the dangdest mess I ever tried to get outside of."

"Well," the friend counseled, "you just get her into a corner some'eres and say to 'er, 'Dearest 'Attie, I hoffer you my 'and hand my 'eart.'"

"But I *can't*," wailed Johnny. "I could never get her into a corner anyway."

"If you can't, you're not hold enough to marry then. What the 'ell would you do with a woman in the 'ouse if you couldn't corner 'er? I tell 'e, women 'ave to 'ave a master, and no man better tackle that job until 'e can be sure 'e can make 'er walk the chalk-line."

"But I don't want her to walk any line; I just want her to speak to me."

"Dang me if I don't believe you are locoed. Why, she's got 'e throwed hand 'og-tied now. What d'e want to make it any worse for?"

They talked for a long time and the Englishman continued to have trouble with his *h*'s; but at last Johnny was encouraged to "corner 'er" next morning before they left for their ranch.

We expected to be astir early anyway, and our curiosity impelled us to see the outcome of the friend's counsel, so we were almost the first in the dining-room next morning. A rather pretty girl was busy arranging the tables, and soon a boyish-looking fellow, wearing great bat-wing chaps, came in and stood warming himself at the stove.

I knew at once it was Johnny, and I saw "'Attie" blush. The very indifference with which she treated him argued well for his cause, but of course he didn't know that. So when she passed by him and her skirt caught on his big spurs they both stooped at once to unfasten it; their heads hit together with such a bump that the ice was broken, although he seemed to think it was her skull. I am sure there ought to be a thaw after all his apologies.

After breakfast Mrs. O'Shaughnessy went out to see her friend Cormac O'Toole. He was the only person in town we could hope to get a team from with which to continue our journey. This is a hard country on horses at best, and at this time of the year particularly so; few will let their teams go out at any price, but Mrs. O'Shaughnessy had hopes, and she is so persuasive that I felt no one could resist her. There was a drummer at breakfast who kept "cussing" the country. He had tried to get a conveyance and had failed; so the cold, the snow, the people, and everything else disgusted him.

Soon Mrs. O'Shaughnessy returned, and as the drummer was trying to get out to E——, and that was our destination also, she made her way toward him, intending to invite him to ride with us. She wore over her best clothes an old coat that had once belonged to someone of her men friends. It had once been bearskin, but was now more *bare* skin, so her appearance was against her; she looked like something with the mange. So Mr. Drummer did not wait to hear what she was going to say but at once exclaimed, "No, madam, I cannot let you ride out with me. I can't get a rig myself in this beastly place." Then he turned to a man standing near and remarked, "These Western women are so bold they don't hesitate to *demand* favours."

Mrs. O'Shaughnessy's eyes fairly snapped, but she said nothing. I think she took a malicious delight in witnessing the drummer's chagrin when a few moments later our comfortable sleigh and good strong team appeared.

We were going to drive ourselves, but we had to drive to the depot for our suit-cases; but when we got there the ticket-office was not open, so the agent was probably having his beauty sleep. There was a fire in the big stove, and we joined the bunch of men in the depot. Among them we noticed a thin, consumptive-looking fellow, evidently a stranger.

Very soon some men began talking of some transaction in which a Bishop B—— was concerned. It seemed they didn't admire the bishop very much; they kept talking of his peculiarities and transgressions, and mentioned his treatment of his wives. His "second," they said, was blind because of cataracts, and, although abundantly able, he left her in darkness. She had never seen her two last children. Some one spoke up and said, "I thought polygamy was no longer practiced." Then the man explained that they no longer contracted plural marriages, but that many kept *all* their wives and B—— still had both of his. He went on to say that although such practice is contrary to law, it was almost impossible to make a case against them, for the women would not swear against their husbands. B—— had been arrested once, but his second swore that she didn't know who her children's father was, and it cost the sheriff his office the next election.

Mrs. O'Shaughnessy spoke to an acquaintance of hers and mentioned where we were going. In a short while we got our suit-cases and we were off, but as we drove past the freight depot, the stranger we had noticed came down the steps and asked us to let him ride out with us. I really felt afraid of him, but Mrs. O'Shaughnessy thinks herself a match for any mere man, so she drew up and the man climbed in. He took the lines and we snuggled down under the robes and listened to the runners, shrill screeching over the frozen surface.

We had dinner with a new settler, and about two o'clock that afternoon we overtook a fellow who was plodding along the road. His name was B——, he said, and he pointed out to us his broad fields and herds. He had been overseeing some feeders he had, and his horse had escaped, so he was walking home, as it was only a couple of miles. He talked a great deal in that two-mile trip; too much for his own good, it developed.

For the first time since B—— climbed into our sleigh, the stranger spoke. "Can you tell me where Mrs. Belle B—— lives?" he asked.

"Why, yes," our passenger replied. "She is a member of our little flock. She is slightly related to me, as you perhaps noticed the name, and I will show you to her house."

"Just how is she related to you?" the stranger asked.

"That," the man replied, "is a matter of protection. I have *given* her

130

the protection of my name."

"Then she is your wife, is she not?" the stranger asked.

"You must be a stranger in this country," the man evaded. "What is your name?"

But the stranger didn't seem to hear, and just then we came opposite the residence of the bishop, and the man we had picked up in the road said, "That is my home, won't you get out and warm? My wife will be glad to get acquainted with you ladies."

We declined, as it was only a short distance to the house of the man Mrs. O'Shaughnessy had come to see, so he stayed in the sleigh to show the stranger to the house of Mrs. Belle B——. I can't say much for it as a house, and I was glad I didn't have to go in. The stranger and B—— got out and entered the house, and we drove away.

Next morning, as we returned through the little village, it was all excitement. Bishop B—— had been shot the night before, just as he had left the house of Mrs. Belle B——, for what reason or by whom no one knew; and if the Bishop knew he had not told, for he either would not or could not talk.

They were going to start with him that day to the hospital, but they had no hopes of his living.

When we came to Mrs. Belle's house, Mrs. O'Shaughnessy got out of the sleigh and went into the house. I could hear her soothing voice, and I was mighty glad the poor, forlorn woman had such a comforter.

★★★★★★

I was so *very* glad to get home. How good it all looked to me! "Poop o' Roome" has a calf, and as we drove up to the corral Clyde was trying to get it into the stall with the rest. It is "Poop's" first calf, and she is very proud of it, and objected to its being put away from her, so she bunted at Clyde, and as he dodged her, the calf ran between his feet and he sat down suddenly in the snow. I laughed at him, but I am powerfully glad he is no follower of old Joseph Smith.

Mrs. Louderer was enjoying herself immensely, she loves children so much. She and Clyde hired the "Tackler"—so called because he will tackle *any* kind of a job, whether he knows anything about it or not—to paper the room. He thinks he is a great judge of the fitness of things and of beauty. The paper has a stripe of roses, so Tackler reversed every other strip so that some of my roses are standing on their heads. Roses don't all grow one way, he claims, and so his method "makes 'em look more nachul like."

A little thing like wallpaper put on upside down don't bother me; but what *would* I do if I were a "second"?

Your loving friend,

Elinore Rupert Stewart.

26

Success

Dear Mrs. Coney,—

This is Sunday and I suppose I ought not to be writing, but I must write to you and I may not have another chance soon. Both your letters have reached me, and now that our questions are settled we can proceed to proceed.

Now, this is the letter I have been wanting to write you for a long time, but could not because until now I had not actually proven all I wanted to prove. Perhaps it will not interest you, but if you see a woman who wants to homestead and is a little afraid she will starve, you can tell her what I am telling you.

I never did like to theorize, and so this year I set out to prove that a woman could ranch if she wanted to. We like to grow potatoes on new ground, that is, newly cleared land on which no crop has been grown. Few weeds grow on new land, so it makes less work. So I selected my potato-patch, and the man ploughed it, although I could have done that if Clyde would have let me. I cut the potatoes, Jerrine helped, and we dropped them in the rows. The man covered them, and that ends the man's part. By that time the garden ground was ready, so I planted the garden. I had almost an acre in vegetables. I irrigated and I cultivated it myself.

We had all the vegetables we could possibly use, and now Jerrine and I have put in our cellar full, and this is what we have: one large bin of potatoes (more than two tons), half a ton of carrots, a large bin of beets, one of turnips, one of onions, one of parsnips, and on the other side of the cellar we have more than one hundred heads of cabbage. I have experimented and found a kind of squash that can be raised here, and that the ripe ones keep well and make good pies; also that the young tender ones make splendid pickles, quite equal to cucumbers. I was glad to stumble on to that, because pickles are hard to manufacture when you have nothing to work with. Now I have plenty.

They told me when I came that I could not even raise common beans, but I tried and succeeded. And also I raised lots of green tomatoes, and, as we like them preserved, I made them all up that way. Experimenting along another line, I found that I could make catchup, as delicious as that of tomatoes, of gooseberries. I made it exactly the same as I do the tomatoes and I am delighted. Gooseberries were very fine and very plentiful this year, so I put up a great many. I milked ten cows twice a day all summer; have sold enough butter to pay for a year's supply of flour and gasoline. We use a gasoline lamp. I have raised enough chickens to completely renew my flock, and all we wanted to eat, and have some fryers to go into the winter with. I have enough turkeys for all of our birthdays and holidays.

I raised a great many flowers and I worked several days in the field. In all I have told about I have had no help but Jerrine. Clyde's mother spends each summer with us, and she helped me with the cooking and the babies. Many of my neighbours did better than I did, although I know many town people would doubt my doing so much, but I did it. I have tried every kind of work this ranch affords, and I can do any of it. Of course I *am* extra strong, but those who try know that strength and knowledge come with doing. I just love to experiment, to work, and to prove out things, so that ranch life and "roughing it" just suit me.

Letters On an Elk Hunt

I HEARD THE REPORT OF GUNS

Contents

1

Connie Willis

Burnt Fork, Wyo., July 8, 1914.

Dear Mrs. Coney,—

Your letter of the 4th just to hand. How glad your letters make me; how glad I am to have you to tell little things to.

I intended to write you as soon as I came back from Green River, to tell you of a girl I saw there; but there was a heap to do and I kept putting it off. I have described the desert so often that I am afraid I will tire you, so I will leave that out and tell you that we arrived in town rather late. The help at the hotel were having their supper in the regular dining-room, as all the guests were out. They cheerfully left their own meal to place ours on the table.

One of them interested me especially. She was a small person; I couldn't decide whether she was a child or a woman. I kept thinking her homely, and then when she spoke I forgot everything but the music of her voice,—it was so restful, so rich and mellow in tone, and she seemed so small for such a splendid voice. Somehow I kept expecting her to squeak like a mouse, but every word she spoke charmed me. Before the meal was over it came out that she was the dish-washer. All the rest of the help had finished their work for the day, but she, of course, had to wash what dishes we had been using.

The rest went their ways; and as our own tardiness had belated her, I offered to help her to carry out the dishes. It was the work of only a moment to dry them, so I did that. She was so small that she had to stand on a box in order to be comfortable while she washed the cups and plates.

"The sink and drain-board were made for real folks. I have to use this box to stand on, or else the water runs back down my sleeves," she told me.

My room was upstairs; she helped me up with the children. She said her name was Connie Willis, that she was the only one of her "ma's first man's" children; but ma married again after pa died and there were a lot of the second batch. When the mother died she left a baby only a few hours old. As Connie was older than the other children she took charge of the household and of the tiny little baby.

I just wish you could have seen her face light up when she spoke of little Lennie.

"Lennie is eight years old now, and she is just as smart as the smartest and as pretty as a doll. All the Ford children are pretty, and smart, too. I am the only homely child ma had. It would do you good just to look at any of the rest, 'specially Lennie."

It certainly did me good to listen to Connie,—her brave patience was so inspiring. As long as I was in town she came every day when her work was finished to talk to me about Lennie. For herself she had no ambition. Her clothes were clean, but they were odds and ends that had served their day for other possessors; her shoes were not mates, and one was larger than the other. She said: "I thought it was a streak of luck when I found the cook always wore out her right shoe first and the dining-room girl the left, because, you see, I could have their old ones and that would save two dollars toward what I am saving up for. But it wasn't so very lucky after all except for the fun, because the cook wears low heels and has a much larger foot than the dining-room girl, who wears high heels. But I chopped the long heel off with the cleaver, and these shoes have saved me enough to buy Lennie a pair of patent-leather slippers to wear on the Fourth of July."

I thought that a foolish ambition, but succeeding conversations made me ashamed of the thought.

I asked her if Lennie's father couldn't take care of her.

"Oh," she said, "Pa Ford is a good man. He has a good heart, but there's so many of them that it is all he can do to rustle what must be had. Why," she told me in a burst of confidence, "I've been saving up for a tombstone for ma for twelve years, but I have to help pa once in a while, and I sometimes think I never will get enough money saved. It is kind of hard on three dollars a week, and then I'm kind of extravagant at times. I have wanted a doll, a beautiful one, all my days. Last Christmas I got it—for Lennie. And then I like to carry out other folks' wishes sometimes. That is what I am fixing to do now. Ma always wanted to see me dressed up real pretty just once, but we were always too poor, and now I'm too old. But I can fix Lennie, and this Fourth of July I am going to put all the beauty on her that ma would have liked to see on me. They always celebrate that day at Manila, Utah, where pa lives. I'll go out and take the things. Then if ma is where she can see, she'll see *one* of her girls dressed for once."

"But aren't you mistaken when you say you have been saving for your mother's tombstone for twelve years? She's only been dead eight."

"Why no, I'm not. You see, at first it wasn't a tombstone but a marble-top dresser. Ma had always wanted one so badly; for she always thought that housekeeping would be so much easier if she had just one pretty thing to keep house toward. If I had not been so selfish, she could have had the dresser before she died. I had fifteen dollars,— enough to buy it,—but when I came to look in the catalogue to choose one I found that for fifteen dollars more I could get a whole set. I thought how proud ma would be of a new bedstead and wash-stand, so I set in to earn that much more. But before I could get that saved up ma just got tired of living, waiting, and doing without. She never caused any trouble while she lived, and she died the same way.

"They sent for me to come home from the place where I was at work. I had just got home, and I was standing by the bed holding ma's hand, when she smiled up at me; she handed me Lennie and then turned over and sighed so contented. That was all there was to it. She was done with hard times.

"Pa Ford wanted to buy her coffin on credit,—to go in debt for it,—but I hated for ma to have to go on that way even after she was dead; so I persuaded him to use what money he had to buy the coffin, and I put in all I had, too. So the coffin she lies in is her own. We don't owe for *that*. Then I stayed at home and kept house and cared for Lennie until she was four years old. I have been washing dishes in this hotel ever since."

That is Connie's story. After she told me, I went to the landlady and suggested that we help a little with Lennie's finery; but she told me to "keep out." "I doubt if Connie would accept any help from us, and if she did, every cent we put in would take that much from her pleasure. There have not been many happy days in her life, but the Fourth of July will be one if we keep out." So I kept out.

I was delighted when Mrs. Pearson invited me to accompany her to Manila to witness the bucking contest on the Fourth. Manila is a pretty little town, situated in Lucerne Valley. All the houses in town are the homes of ranchers, whose farms may be seen from any doorstep in Manila. The valley lies between a high wall of red sandstone and the "hogback,"—that is what the foothills are called. The wall of sandstone is many miles in length. The valley presents a beautiful picture as you go eastward; at this time of the year the alfalfa is so green. Each farm joins another. Each has a cabin in which the rancher lives while they irrigate and make hay. When that is finished they move into their houses in "town." Beyond the hogback rise huge mountains, rugged *cañons*, and noisy mountain streams; great forests of pine help to make up the picture. Looking toward the east we could see where mighty Green River cuts its way through walls of granite. The road lies close up against the sandstone and cedar hills and along the canal that carries the water to all the farms in the valley. I enjoyed every moment. It was all so beautiful,—the red rock, the green fields, the warm brown sand of the road and bare places, the mighty mountains, the rugged cedars and sage-brush spicing the warm air, the blue distance and the fleecy clouds. Oh, I wish I could paint it for you! In the foreground there should be some cows being driven home by a barefooted boy with a gun on his shoulder and a limp brown rabbit in his hand. But I shall have to leave that to your imagination and move on to the Fourth.

On that day every one turns out; even from the very farthest outlying ranches they come, and every one dressed in his best. No matter what privation is suffered all the rest of the time, on this day everyone is dressed to kill. Every one has a little money with which to buy gaudy boxes of candy; every girl has a chew of gum. Among the children friendship is proved by invitations to share lemons. They cordially invite each other to "come get a suck o' my lemon." I just *love* to watch them. Old and young are alike; whatever may trouble them at other times is forgotten, and everyone dances, eats candy, sucks lemons, laughs, and makes merry on the Fourth.

I didn't care much for their contests. I was busy watching the faces. Soon I saw one I knew. Connie was making her way toward me. I wondered how I could ever have thought her plain. Pride lighted every feature. She led by the hand the most beautiful child I have ever seen. She is a few weeks younger than Jerrine[1] but much smaller. She had such an elusive beauty that I cannot describe it. One not acquainted with her story might have thought her dress out of taste out among the sand dunes and sage-brush in the hot sun, but I knew, and I felt the thrill of sheer blue silk, dainty patent-leather slippers, and big

1. The author's daughter aged 8.

blue hat just loaded with pink rose-buds.

"This is my Lennie," said Connie proudly.

I saw all the Ford family before I left,—the weak-faced, discouraged-looking father and the really beautiful girls. Connie was neat in a pretty little dress, cheap but becoming, and her shoes were mates. Lennie was the centre of family pride. She represented all their longings.

Before I left, Connie whispered to me that she would very soon have money enough to pay for her mother's tombstone. "Then I will have had everything I ever wanted. I guess I won't have anything else to live for then; I guess I will have to get to wanting something for Lennie."

On our way home even the mosquito bites didn't annoy me; I was too full of Connie's happiness. All my happiness lacked was your presence. If I had had you beside me to share the joy and beauty, I could have asked for nothing more. I kept saying, "How Mrs. Coney would enjoy this!" All I can do is to kind of hash it over for you. I hope you like hash.

With much love to you,

Elinore.

2

The Start

In Camp on the Desert,
August 24, 1914.

Dear Mrs. Coney,—

At last we are off. I am powerfully glad. I shall have to enjoy this trip for us both. You see how greedy I am for new experiences! I have never been on a prolonged hunt before, so I am looking forward to a heap of fun. I hardly know what to do about writing, but shall try to write every two days. I want you to have as much of this trip as I can put on paper, so we will begin at the start.

To begin with we were all to meet at Green River, to start the twentieth; but a professor coming from somewhere in the East delayed us a day, and also some of the party changed their plans; that reduced our number but not our enthusiasm.

A few days before we left the ranch I telephoned Mrs. Louderer and tried to persuade her to go along, but she replied, "For why should I go? Vat? Iss it to freeze? I can sleep out on some rocks here and with a stick I can beat the sage-bush, which will give me the smell you will smell of the outside. And for the game I can have a beef kill which iss better to eat as elk."

I love Mrs. Louderer dearly, but she is absolutely devoid of imagination, and her matter-of-factness is mighty trying sometimes. However, she sent me a bottle of goose-grease to ward off colds from the "*kinder*."

I tried Mrs. O'Shaughnessy, but she was plumb aggravating and non-committal, and it seemed when we got to Green River that I would be the only woman in the party. Besides, all the others were strangers to me except young Mr. Haynes, who was organising the hunt. Really the prospect didn't seem so joyous.

The afternoon before we were to start I went with Mr. Stewart and Mr. Haynes to meet the train. We were expecting the professor. But the only passenger who got off was a slight, gray-eyed girl. She looked about her uncertainly for a moment and then went into the depot while we returned to the hotel. Just as I started up the steps my eyes were gladdened by the sight of Mrs. O'Shaughnessy in her buckboard trotting merrily up the street. She waved her hand to us and drove up. Clyde took her team to the livery barn and she came up to my room with me.

"It's going with you I am," she began. "Ye'll need somebody to keep yez straight and to sew up the holes ye'll be shooting into each other."

After she had "tidied up a bit" we went down to supper. We were all seated at one table, and there was yet an empty place; but soon the girl we had seen get off the train came and seated herself in it.

"Can any of you tell me how to get to Kendall, Wyoming?" she asked.

I didn't know nor did Clyde, but Mrs. O'Shaughnessy knew, so she answered. "Kendall is in the forest reserve up north. It is two hundred miles from here and half of the distance is across desert, but they have an automobile route as far as Pinedale; you could get that far on the auto stage. After that I suppose you could get some one to take you on."

"Thank you," said the girl. "My name is Elizabeth Hull. I am alone in the world, and I am not expected at Kendall, so I am obliged to ask and to take care of myself."

Mrs. O'Shaughnessy at once mentioned her own name and introduced the rest of us. After supper Miss Hull and Mrs. O'Shaughnessy had a long talk. I was not much surprised when Mrs. O'Shaughnessy came in to tell me that she was going to take the girl along. "Because," she said, "Kendall is on our way and it's glad I am to help a lone girl. Did you notice the freckles of her? Sure her forbears hailed from Killarney."

So early next morning we were astir. We had outfitted in Green River, so the wagons were already loaded. I had rather dreaded the professor. I had pictured to myself a very dignified, bespectacled person, and I mentally stood in awe of his great learning. Imagine my surprise when a boyish, laughing young man introduced himself as Professor Glenholdt. He was so jolly, so unaffected, and so altogether likable, that my fear vanished and I enjoyed the prospect of his com-

145

pany. Mr. Haynes and his friend Mr. Struble on their wagon led the way, then we followed, and after us came Mrs. O'Shaughnessy, and Miss Hull brought up the rear, with the professor riding horseback beside first one wagon and then another.

So we set out. There was a great jangling and banging, for our tin camp-stoves kept the noise going. Neither the children nor I can ride under cover on a wagon, we get so sick; so there we were, perched high up on great rolls of bedding and a tent. I reckon we looked funny to the "onlookers looking on" as we clattered down the street; but we were off and that meant a heap.

All the morning our way lay up the beautiful river, past the great red cliffs and through tiny green parks, but just before noon the road wound itself up on to the mesa, which is really the beginning of the desert. We crowded into the shadow of the wagons to eat our midday meal; but we could not stop long, because it was twenty-eight miles to where we could get water for the horses when we should camp that night. So we wasted no time.

Shortly after noon we could see white clouds of alkali dust ahead. By and by we came up with the dust-raisers. The children and I had got into the buckboard with Mrs. O'Shaughnessy and Miss Hull, so as to ride easier and be able to gossip, and we had driven ahead of the wagons, so as to avoid the stinging dust.

The sun was just scorching when we overtook the funniest layout I have seen since Cora Belle[1] drove up to our door the first time. In a wobbly old buckboard sat a young couple completely engrossed by each other. That he was a Westerner we knew by his cowboy hat and boots; that she was an Easterner, by her not knowing how to dress for the ride across the desert. She wore a foolish little chiffon hat which the alkali dust had ruined, and all the rest of her clothes matched. But over them the enterprising young man had raised one of those big old sunshades that had lettering on them. It kept wobbling about in the socket he had improvised; one minute we could see "Tea"; then a rut in the road would swing "Coffee" around. Their sunshade kept revolving about that way, and sometimes their heads revolved a little bit, too. We could hear a word occasionally and knew they were having a great deal of fun at our expense; but we were amused ourselves, so we didn't care. They would drive along slowly until we almost reached them; then they would whip up and raise such a dust that we were almost choked.

1. The story of Cora Belle is told in *Letters of a Woman Homesteader.*

Mrs. O'Shaughnessy determined to drive ahead; so she trotted up alongside, but she could not get ahead. The young people were giggling. Mrs. O'Shaughnessy doesn't like to be the joke all the time. Suddenly she leaned over toward them and said: "Will ye tell me something?" Oh, yes, they would. "Then," she said, "which of you are Tea and which Coffee?"

Their answer was to drive up faster and stir up a powerful lot of dust. They kept pretty well ahead after that, but at sundown we came up with them at the well where we were to camp. This well had been sunk by the county for the convenience of travellers, and we were mighty thankful to find it. It came out that our young couple were bride and groom. They had never seen each other until the night before, having met through a matrimonial paper. They had met in Green River and were married that morning, and the young husband was taking her away up to Pinedale to his ranch.

They must have been ideally happy, for they had forgotten their mess-box, and had only a light lunch. They had only their lap-robe for bedding. They were in a predicament; but the girl's chief concern was lest "Honey-bug" should let the wolves get her. Though it is scorching hot on the desert by day, the nights are keenly cool, and I was wondering how they would manage with only their lap-robe, when Mrs. O'Shaughnessy, who cannot hold malice, made a round of the camp, getting a blanket here and a coat there, until she had enough to make them comfortable. Then she invited them to take their meals with us until they could get to where they could help themselves.

I think we all enjoyed camp that night, for we were all tired. We were in a shallow little *cañon*,—not a tree, not even a bush except sagebrush. Luckily, there was plenty of that, so we had roaring fires. We sat around the fire talking as the blue shadows faded into gray dusk and the big stars came out. The newly-weds were, as the bride put it, "so full of happiness they had nothing to put it in." Certainly their spirits overflowed. They were eager to talk of themselves and we didn't mind listening.

They are Mr. and Mrs. Tom Burney. She is the oldest of a large family of children and has had to "work out ever since she was big enough to get a job." The people she had worked for rather frowned upon any matrimonial ventures, and as no provision was made for "help" entertaining company, she had never had a "*beau*." One day she got hold of a matrimonial paper and saw Mr. Burney's ad. She answered and they corresponded for several months. We were just in time to "catch it,"

147

as Mr. Haynes—who is a confirmed bachelor—disgustedly remarked. Personally, I am glad; I like them much better than I thought I should when they were raising so much dust so unnecessarily.

I must close this letter, as I see the men are about ready to start. The children are standing the trip well, except that Robert is a little sun-blistered. Did I tell you we left Junior with his grandmother? Even though I have the other three, my heart is hungry for my "big boy," who is only a baby, too. He is such a precious little man. I wish you could see him!

With a heart very full of love for you,

E. R. S.

3

Eden Valley

In Camp, August 28.

Dear Mrs. Coney,—

We are almost across the desert, and I am really becoming interested. The difficulties some folks work under are enough to make many of us ashamed. In the very centre of the desert is a little settlement called Eden Valley. Imagination must have had a heap to do with its name, but one thing is certain: the serpent will find the crawling rather bad if he attempts to enter *this* Eden, for the sand is hot; the alkali and the cactus are there, so it must be a serpentless Eden. The settlers have made a long canal and bring their water many miles. They say the soil is splendid, and they don't have much stone; but it is such a flat place! I wonder how they get the water to run when they irrigate.

We saw many deserted homes. Hope's skeletons they are, with their yawning doors and windows like eyeless sockets. Some of the houses, which looked as if they were deserted, held families. We camped near one such. Mrs. O'Shaughnessy and I went up to the house to buy some eggs. A hopeless-looking woman came to the door. The hot winds and the alkali dust had tanned her skin and bleached her hair; both were a gray-brown. Her eyes were blue, but were so tired-looking that I could hardly see for the tears.

"No," she said, "we ain't got no eggs. We ain't got no chickens. You see this ground is sandy, and last year the wind blowed awful hard and all the grain blowed out, so we didn't have no chance to raise chickens. We had no feed and no money to buy feed, so we had to kill our chickens to save their lives. We et 'em. They would have starved anyway."

Then we tried for some vegetables. "Well she said, "they ain't much to look at; maybe you'll not want 'em. Our garden ain't much this

149

year. Pa has had to work out all the time. The kids and me put in some seed—all we had—with a hoe. We ain't got no horse; our team died last winter. We didn't have much feed and it was shore a hard winter. We hated to see old Nick and Fanny die. They were just like ones of the family. We drove 'em clean from Missouri, too. But they died, and what hurt me most was, pa 'lowed it would be a turrible waste not to skin 'em. I begged him not to. Land knows the pore old things was entitled to their hides, they got so little else; but pa said it didn't make no difference to them whether they had any hide or not, and that the skins would sell for enough to get the kids some shoes. And they did. A Jew junk man came through and give pa three dollars for the two hides, and that paid for a pair each for Johnny and Eller.

"Pa hated as bad as we did to lose our faithful old friends, and all the winter long we grieved, the kids and me. Every time the coyotes yelped we knew they were gathering to gnaw poor old Nick and Fan's bones. And pa, to keep from crying himself when the kids and me would be sobbin', would scold us. 'My goodness,' he would say, 'the horses are dead and they don't know nothin' about cold and hunger. They don't know nothin' about sore shoulders and hard pulls now, so why don't you shut up and let them and me rest in peace?' But that was only pa's way of hidin' the tears.

"When spring came the kids and me gathered all the bones and hair we could find of our good old team, and buried 'em where you see that green spot. That's grass. We scooped all the trash out of the mangers, and spread it over the grave, and the timothy and the redtop seed in the trash came up and growed. I'd liked to have put some flowers there, but we had no seed."

She wiped her face on her apron, and gathered an armful of cabbage; it had not headed but was the best she had. Mrs. O'Shaughnessy seemed possessed; she bought stuff she knew she would have to throw away, but she didn't offer one word of sympathy. I felt plumb out of patience with her, for usually she can say the most comforting things.

"Why don't you leave this place? Why not go away somewhere else, where it will not be so hard to start?" I asked.

"Oh, 'cause pa's heart is just set on making a go of it here, and we would be just as pore anywhere else. We have tried a heap of times to start a home, and we've worked hard, but we were never so pore before. We have been here three years and we can prove up soon; then maybe we can go away and work somewhere, enough to get a team anyway. Pa has already worked out his water-right,—he's got water for all his land paid for, if we only had a team to plough with. But we'll get it. Pa's been workin' all summer in the hay, and he ought to have a little stake saved. Then the sheep-men will be bringin' in their herds soon's frost comes and pa 'lows to get a job herdin'. Anyway, we got to stick. We ain't got no way to get away and all we got is right here. Every last dollar we had has went into improvin' this place. If pore old hard-worked pa can stand it, the kids and me can. We ain't seen pa for two months, not sence hayin' began, but we work all we can to shorten the days; and we sure do miss pore old Nick and Fan."

We gathered up as much of the vegetables as we could carry. Mrs. O'Shaughnessy paid, and we started homeward, promising to send for the rest of the beets and potatoes. On the way we met two children, and knew them at once for "Johnny and Eller." They had pails, and were carrying water from the stream and pouring it on the green spot that covered Nick and Fan. We promised them each a dime if they would bring the vegetables we had left. Their little faces shone, and we had to hurry all we could to get supper ready before they came; for we were determined they should eat supper with us.

We told the men before the little tykes came. So Mr. Struble let Johnny shoot his gun and both youngsters rode Chub and Antifat to water. They were bright little folks and their outlook upon life is not so flat and colourless as their mother's is. A day holds a world of chance for them. They were saving their money, they told us, "to buy some house plants for ma." Johnny had a dollar which a sheep-man had given him for taking care of a sore-footed dog. Ella had a dime which a man had given her for filling his water-bag. They both hoped to pull wool off dead sheep and make some more money that way. They had quite made up their minds about what they wanted to get: it must be house plants for ma; but still they both wished they could get some little thing for pa. They were not pert or forward in any way, but they answered readily and we all drew them out, even the newly-weds.

After supper the men took their guns and went out to shoot sage-hens. Johnny went with Mr. Haynes and Mr. Struble. Miss Hull walked back with Ella, and we sent Mrs. Sanders a few cans of fruit. Mrs. O'Shaughnessy and I washed the dishes. We were talking of the Sanders family. Mrs. O'Shaughnessy was disgusted with me because I wept.

"You think it is a soft heart you have, but it is only your head that is soft. Of course they are having a hard time. What of it? The very root

151

of independence is hard times. That's the way America was founded; that is why it stands so firmly. Hard times is what makes sound characters. And them kids are getting a new hold on character that was very near run to seed in the parents. Johnny will be tax-assessor yet, I'll bet you, and you just watch that Eller. It won't surprise me a bit to see her county superintendent of schools. The parents most likely never would make anything; but having just only a pa and a ma and getting the very hard licks them kids are getting now, is what is going to make them something more than a pa and a ma."

Mrs. O'Shaughnessy is very wise, but sometimes she seems absolutely heartless.

The men didn't bring back much game; each had left a share with Mrs. Sanders.

Next morning we were astir early. We pulled out of camp just as the first level rays of the sun shot across the desolate, flat country. We crossed the flat little stream with its soft sandy banks. A willow here and there along the bank and the blue, distant mountains and some lonesome buttes were all there was to break the monotony. Yet we saw some prosperous-looking places with many haystacks. I looked back once toward the Sanders cabin. The blue smoke was just beginning to curl upward from the stove pipe. The green spot looked vividly green against the dim prospect. Poor pa and poor ma! Even if they could be *nothing* more, I wish at least that they need not have given up Nick and Fan!

Mr. Haynes told us at breakfast that we would camp only one more night on the desert. I am so glad of that. The newly-weds will leave us in two more days. I'm rather sorry; they are much nicer than I thought they would be. They have invited us to stay with them on our way back. Well, I must stop. I wish I could put some of this clean morning air inside your apartments.

With much love,

E. R. S.

4

Crazy Olaf and Others

In Camp, August 31, 1914.

Dear Mrs. Coney,—

We are across the desert, and camped for a few days' fishing on a shady, bowery little stream. We have had two frosty nights and there are trembling golden groves on every hand. Four men joined us at Newfork, and the bachelors have gone on; but Mr. Stewart wanted to rest the "beasties" and we all wanted to fish, so we camped for a day or two.

The twenty-eighth was the warmest day we have had, the most disagreeable in every way. Not a breath of air stirred except an occasional whirlwind, which was hot and threw sand and dust over us. We could see the heat glimmering, and not a tree nor a green spot. The mountains looked no nearer. I am afraid we *all* rather wished we were at home. Water was getting very scarce, so the men wanted to reach by noon a long, low valley they knew of; for sometimes water could be found in a buried river-bed there, and they hoped to find enough for the horses. But a little after noon we came to the spot, and only dry, glistening sand met our eyes. The men emptied the water-bags for the horses; they all had a little water. We had to be saving, so none of us washed our dust-grimed faces.

We were sitting in the scant shadow of the wagons eating our dinner when we were startled to see a tall, bare-headed man come racing down the draw. His clothes and shoes were in tatters; there were great blisters on his arms and shoulders where the sun had burned him; his eyes were swollen and red, and his lips were cracked and bloody. His hair was so white and so dusty that altogether he was a pitiful-looking object. He greeted us pleasantly, and said that his name was Olaf Swanson and that he was a sheep-herder; that he had seen us and had come to ask for a little smoking. By that he meant tobacco.

Mrs. O'Shaughnessy was eyeing him very closely. She asked him when he had eaten. That morning, he said. She asked him *what* he had eaten; he told her cactus balls and a little rabbit. I saw her exchange glances with Professor Glenholdt, and she left her dinner to get out her war-bag.

She called Olaf aside and gently dressed his blisters with Listerine; after she had helped him to clean his mouth she said to him, "Now, Olaf, sit by me and eat; show me how much you can eat. Then tell me what you mean by saying you are a sheep-herder; don't you think we know there will be no sheep on the desert before there is snow to make water for them?"

"I am what I say I am," he said. "I am not herding now because sorrow has drove me to dig wells. It is sorrow for horses. Have you not seen their bones every mile or so along this road? Them's markers. Every pile of bones marks where man's most faithful friend has laid down at last: most of 'em died in the harness and for want of water.

"I killed a horse once. I was trying to have a good time. I had been out with sheep for months and hadn't seen any one but my pardner. We planned to have a rippin' good time when we took the sheep in off the summer range and drew our pay. You don't know how people-hungry a man gets livin' out. So my pardner and me layed out to have one spree. We had a neat little bunch of money, but when we got to town we felt lost as sheep. We didn't know nobody but the bartender. We kept taking a drink now and then just so as to have him to talk to. Finally, he told us there was going to be a dance that night, so we asked around and found we could get tickets for two dollars each. Sam said he'd like to go. We bought tickets.

"Somehow or another they knew us for sheep-herders, and every once in a while somebody would *baa-baa* at us. We had a couple of dances, but after that we couldn't get a pardner. After midnight things begun to get pretty noisy. Sam and me was settin' wonderin' if we were havin' a good time, when a fellow stepped on Sam's foot and said *baa*. I rose up and was goin' to smash him, but Sam collared me and said, 'Let's get away from here, Olaf, before trouble breaks out.' It sounded as if every man in the house and some of the women were *baa*-ing.

"We were pretty near the door when a man put his hand to his nose and *baa*-ed. I knocked him down, and before you could bat your eye everybody was fightin'. We couldn't get out, so we backed into a corner; and every man my fist hit rested on the floor till somebody helped him away. A fellow hit me on the head with a chair and I didn't know how I finished or got out.

"The first thing I remember after that was feeling the greasewood thorns tearing my flesh and my clothes next day. We were away out on the desert not far from North Pilot butte. Poor Sam couldn't speak. I got him off poor old Pinto, and took off the saddle for a pillow for him. I hung the saddle-blanket on a greasewood so as to shade his face; then I got on my own poor horse, poor old Billy, and started to hunt help. I rode and rode. I was tryin' to find some outfit. When Billy lagged I beat him on. You see, I was thinking of Sam. After a while the horse staggered,—stepped into a badger hole, I thought. But he kept staggerin'. I fell off on one side just as he pitched forward. He tried and tried to get up. I stayed till he died; then I kept walking. I don't know what became of Sam; I don't know what became of me; but I do know I am going to dig wells all over this desert until every thirsty horse can have water."

All the time he had been eating just pickles; when he finished his story he ate faster. By now we all knew he was demented. The men tried to coax him to go on with us so that they could turn him over to the authorities, but he said he must be digging. At last it was decided to send someone back for him. Mr. Struble was unwilling to leave him, but the man would not be persuaded. Suddenly he gathered up his "smoking" and some food and ran back up the draw. We had to go on, of course.

All that afternoon our road lay along the buried river. I don't mean dry river. Sand had blown into the river until the water was buried. Water was only a few feet down, and the banks were clearly defined. Sometimes we came to a small, dirty puddle, but it was so alkaline that nothing could drink it. The story we had heard had saddened us all, and we were sorry for our horses. Poor little Elizabeth Hull wept. She said the West was so big and bare, and she was so alone and so sad, she just *had* to cry.

About sundown we came to a ranch and were made welcome by one Timothy Hobbs, owner of the place. The dwelling and the stables were a collection of low brown houses, made of logs and daubed with mud. Fields of shocked grain made a very prosperous-looking background. A belled cow led a bunch of sleek cattle home over the sand dunes. A well in the yard afforded plenty of clear, cold water, which was raised by a windmill. The cattle came and drank at the trough, the bell making a pleasant sound in the twilight.

The men told Mr. Hobbs about the man we saw. "Oh, yes," he said, "that is Crazy Olaf. He has been that way for twenty years. Spends his time digging wells, but he never gets any water, and the sand caves in almost as fast as he can get it out." Then he launched upon a recital of how he got sweet water by piping past the alkali *strata*. I kept hoping he would tell how Olaf was kept and who was responsible for him, but he never told.

He invited us to prepare our supper in his kitchen, and as it was late and wood was scarce, we were glad to accept. He bustled about helping us, adding such dainties as fresh milk, butter, and eggs to our menu. He is a rather stout little man, with merry gray eyes and brown hair beginning to gray. He wore a red shirt and blue overalls, and he wiped his butcher's knife impartially on the legs of his overalls or his towel,—just whichever was handiest as he hurried about cutting our bacon and opening cans for us.

Mrs. O'Shaughnessy and he got on famously. After supper, while she and Elizabeth washed the dishes, she asked him why he didn't get married and have someone to look after him and his cabin.

"I don't have time," he answered. "I came West eighteen years ago to make a start and a home for Jennie and me, but I can't find time to go back and get her. In the summer I have to hustle to make the hay and grain, and I have to stay and feed the stock all the rest of the time."

"You write her once in a while, don't you?" asked Mrs. O'Shaughnessy.

"Yes," he said, "I wrote her two years ago come April; then I was so busy I didn't go to town till I went for my year's supplies. I went to the post office, and sure enough there was a letter for me,—been waitin' for me for six months. You see the postmaster knows me and never would send a letter back. I set down there right in the office and answered it. I told her how it was, told her I was coming after her soon as I could find time. You see, she refuses to come to me 'cause I am so far from the railroad, and she is afraid of Indians and wild animals."

"Have you got your answer?" asked Elizabeth.

"No," he said, "I ain't had time yet to go, but I kind of wish somebody would think to bring the mail. Not many people pass here, only when the open season takes hunters to the mountains. When you people come back will you stop and ask for the mail for me?"

We promised.

In the purple and amber light of a new day we were about, and soon were on the road. By nightfall we had bidden the desert a glad farewell, and had camped on a large stream among trees. How glad we were to see so much water and such big cottonwoods! Mr. and Mrs. Burney were within a day's drive of home, so they left us. This camp is at Newfork, and our party has four new members: a doctor, a moving-picture man, and two geological fellows. They have gone on, but we will join them soon.

Just across the creek from us is the cabin of a new settler. Mrs. O'Shaughnessy and I slept together last night,—only we couldn't sleep for the continual, whining cry of a sick baby at the cabin. So after a while we rose and dressed and crossed over to see if we could be of any help. We found a woefully distressed young couple. Their first child, about a year old, was very sick. They didn't know what to do for it; and she was afraid to stay alone while he went for help.

They were powerfully glad to see us, and the young father left at once to get Grandma Mortimer, a neighbourhood godsend such as most Western communities have one of. We busied ourselves relieving the young mother as much as we could. She wouldn't leave the baby and lie down. The child is teething and had convulsions. We put it into a hot bath and held the convulsions in check until Mrs. Mortimer came. She bustled in and took hold in a way to insure confidence. She had not been there long before she had both parents in bed, "saving themselves for tomorrow," and was gently rubbing the hot little body of the baby. She kept giving it warm tea she had made of herbs, until soon the threatening jerks were over, the peevish whining ceased, and the child slept peacefully on Grandma's lap. I watched her, fascinated. There was never a bit of faltering, no indecision; everything she did seemed exactly what she ought to do.

"How did you learn it all?" I asked her. "How can you know just what to do, and then have the courage to do it? I should be afraid of doing the wrong thing."

"Why," she said, "that is easy. Just do the very best you can and trust God for the rest. After all, it is God who saves the baby, not us and not our efforts; but we can help. He lets us do that. Lots of times the good we do goes beyond any medicine. Never be afraid to *help* your best. I have been doing that for forty years and I am going to keep it up till I die."

Then she told us story after story—told us how her different ambitions had "boosted" her along, had made her swim when she just

157

wanted to float. "I was married when I was sixteen, and of course, my first ambition was to own a home for Dave. My man was poor. He had a horse, and his folks gave him another. My father gave me a heifer, and mother fitted me out with a bed. That was counted a pretty good start then, but we would have married even if we hadn't had one thing. Being young we were over-hopeful. We both took to work like a duck to water. Some years it looked as if we were going to see every dream come true. Another time and we would be poorer than at first. One year the hail destroyed everything; another time the flood carried away all we had.

"When little Dave was eleven years old, he had learned to plough. Every one of us was working to our limit that year. I ploughed and hoed, both, and big Dave really hardly took time to sleep. You see, his idea was that we must do better by our children than we had been done by, and Fanny, our eldest, was thirteen. Big Dave thought all girls married at sixteen because his mother did, and so did I; so that spring he said, 'In just three years Fanny will be leaving us and we *must* do right by her. I wanted powerfully bad that *you* should have a blue silk wedding dress, mother, but of course it couldn't be had, and you looked as pretty as a rose in your pink lawn. But I've always wanted you to have a blue silk. As you can't have it, let us get it for Fanny; and of course we must have everything else according.' And so we worked mighty hard.

"Little Dave begged to be allowed to plough. Every other boy in the neighbourhood did,—some of them younger than he,—but somehow I didn't want him to. One of our neighbours had been sick a lot that year and his crops were about ruined. It was laying-by time and we had finished laying by our crops—all but about half a day's ploughing in the corn. That morning at breakfast, big Dave said he would take the horses and go over to Henry Boles's and plough that day to help out,—said he could finish ours any time, and it didn't matter much if it didn't get ploughed. He told the children to lay off that day and go fishing and berrying. So he went to harness his team, and little Dave went to help him. Fanny and I went to milk, and all the time I could hear little Dave begging his father to let him finish the ploughing. His father said he could if I said so.

"I will never forget his eager little face as he began on me. He had a heap of freckles; I remember noticing them that morning; he was barefooted, and I remember that one toe was skinned. Big Dave was lighting his pipe, and till today I remember how he looked as he held the match to his pipe, drew a puff of smoke, and said, 'Say yes, mother.' So I said yes, and little Dave ran to open the gate for his father.

"As big Dave rode through the gate, our boy caught him by the leg and said, 'I just *love* you, daddy.' Big Dave bent down and kissed him, and said, 'You're a *man*, son.' How proud that made the little fellow! Parents should praise their children more; the little things work hard for a few words of praise, and many of them never get their pay.

"Well, the little fellow would have no help to harness his mule; so Fanny and I went to the house, and Fanny said, 'We ought to cook an extra good dinner to celebrate Davie's first ploughing. I'll go down in the pasture and gather some blackberries if you will make a cobbler.'

"She was gone all morning. About ten o'clock, I took a pail of fresh water down to the field. I knew Davie would be thirsty, and I was uneasy about him, but he was all right. He pushed his ragged old hat back and wiped the sweat from his brow just as his father would have done. I petted him a little, but he was so mannish he didn't want me to pet him any more. After he drank, he took up his lines again, and said, 'Just watch me, mother; see how I can plough.' I told him that we were going to have chicken and dumplings for dinner, and that he must sit in his father's place and help us to berry-cobbler. As he had only a few more rows to plough, I went back, telling myself how foolish I had been to be afraid.

"Twelve o'clock came, but not Davie. I sent Fanny to the spring for the buttermilk and waited a while, thinking little Dave had not finished as soon as he had expected. I went to the field. Little Dave lay on his face in the furrow. I gathered him up in my arms; he was yet alive; he put one weak little arm around my neck, and said, 'Oh, mammy, I'm hurt. The mule kicked me in the stomach.'

"I don't know how I got to the house with him; I stumbled over clods and weeds, through the hot sunshine. I sank down on the porch in the shade, with the precious little form clasped tightly to me. He smiled, and tried to speak, but the blood gurgled up into his throat and my little boy was gone.

"I would have died of grief if I hadn't had to work so hard. Big Dave got too warm at work that day, and when Fanny went for him and told him about little Dave, he ran all the way home; he was crazy with grief and forgot the horses. The trouble and the heat and the overwork brought on a fever. I had no time for tears for three months, and by that time my heart was hardened against my Maker. I got deeper in the rut of work, but I had given up my ambition for a home of my own; all I wanted to do was to work so hard that I could not think of the little grave on which the leaves were falling. I wanted, too, to save enough money to mark the precious spot, and then I wanted to leave. But first one thing and then another took every dollar we made for three years.

"One morning big Dave looked so worn out and pale that I said, 'I am going to get out of here; I am not going to stay here and bury *you*, Dave. Sunrise tomorrow will see us on the road West. We have worked for eighteen years as hard as we knew how, and have given up my boy besides; and now we can't even afford to mark his grave decently. It is time we left.'

"Big Dave went back to bed, and I went out and sold what we had. It was so little that it didn't take long to sell it. That was years ago. We came West. The country was really wild then; there was a great deal of lawlessness. We didn't get settled down for several years; we hired to a man who had a contract to put up hay for the government, and we worked for him for a long time.

"Indians were thick as fleas on a dog then; some were camped near us once, and among them was a Mexican woman who could jabber a little English. Once, when I was feeling particularly resentful and sorrowful, I told her about my little Dave; and it was her jabbered words that showed me the way to peace. I wept for hours, but peace had come and has stayed. Ambition came again, but a different kind: I wanted the same peace to come to all hearts that came so late to mine, and I wanted to help bring it. I took the only course I knew. I have gone to others' help every time there has been a chance. After Fanny married and Dave died, I had an ambition to save up four hundred dollars with which to buy an entrance into an old ladies' home. Just before I got the full amount saved up, I found that young Eddie Carwell wanted to enter the ministry and needed help to go to college. I had just enough; so I gave it to him.

"Another time I had almost enough, when Charlie Rucker got into trouble over some mortgage business; so I used what I had that time to help him. Now I've given up the old ladies' home idea and am saving up for the blue silk dress Dave would have liked me to have. I guess I'll die some day and I want it to be buried in. I like to think I'm going to my two Daves then; and it won't be hard,—especially if I have the blue silk on."

Just then a sleepy little bird twittered outside, and the baby stirred a little. The first faint light of dawn was just creeping up the valley. I rose and said I must get back to camp. Mrs. O'Shaughnessy and I had both wept with Mrs. Mortimer over little Dave. We have all given up our first-born little man-child; so we felt near each other. We told Mrs. Mortimer that we had passed under the rod also. I kissed her toilworn old hands, and Mrs. O'Shaughnessy dropped a kiss on her old gray head as we passed out into the rose-and-gold morning. We felt that we were leaving a sanctified presence, and we are both of us better and humbler women because we met a woman who has buried her sorrow beneath faith and endeavour.

This doesn't seem much like a letter, does it? When I started on this trip, I resolved that you should have just as much of the trip as I could give you. I didn't know we would be so long getting to the hunting-ground, and I felt you would *like* to know of the people we meet. Perhaps my next letter will not be so tame. The hunting season opens tomorrow, but we are several days' travel from the elk yet.

Elizabeth behaves queerly. She doesn't want to go on, stay here, or go back. I am perfectly mystified. So far she has not told us a thing, and we don't know to whom she is going or anything about it. She is a likable little lady, and I sincerely hope she knows what she is doing. It is bedtime and I must stop writing. We go on tomorrow.

  With affectionate regards,

           Elinore Rupert Stewart.

5

Danyul and His Mother

In Camp on the Gros Ventre,
September 6, 1914.

My Dear Friend,—

I have neglected you for almost a week, but when you read this letter and learn why, I feel sure you will forgive me.

To begin with, we bade Mrs. Mortimer goodbye, and started out to find better fishing than the pretty little stream we were on afforded us. Our way lay up Green River and we were getting nearer our final camp-ground all the time, but we were in no hurry to begin hunting, so we were just loitering along. There were a great many little lakes along the valley, and thousands of duck. Mr. Stewart was driving, but as he wanted to shoot ducks, I took the lines and drove along. There is so much that is beautiful, and I was trying so hard to see it all, that I took the wrong road; but none of us noticed it at first, and then we didn't think it worth while to turn back.

The road we were on had lain along the foothills, but when I first thought I had missed the right road we were coming down into a grassy valley. Mr. Stewart came across a marshy stretch of meadow and climbed up on the wagon. The ground was more level, and on every side were marshes and pools; the willows grew higher here so that we couldn't see far ahead. Mrs. O'Shaughnessy was behind, and she called out, "Say, I believe we are off the road." Elizabeth said she had noticed a road winding off on our right; so we agreed that I must have taken the wrong one, but as we couldn't turn in the willows, we had to go on. Soon we reached higher, drier ground and passed through a yellow grove of quaking asp.

A man came along with an axe on his shoulder, and Mr. Stewart asked him about the road. "Yes," he said, "you are off the main road, but on a better. You'll cross the same stream you were going to camp on, right at my ranch. It is just a little way across here and it's almost sundown, so I will show you the way."

He strode along ahead. We drove through an avenue of great dark pines and across a log bridge that spanned a noisy, brawling stream. The man opened a set of bars and we drove into a big clean corral. Comfortable sheds and stables lined one side, and big stacks of hay were conveniently placed. He began to help unharness the teams, saying that they might just as well run in his meadow, as he was through haying; then the horses would be safe while we fished. He insisted on our stopping in his cabin, which we found to be a comfortable two-room affair with a veranda the whole length. The *biggest* pines overshadowed the house; just behind it was a garden, in which some late vegetables were still growing. The air was rather frosty and some worried hens were trying hard to cover some chirping half-feathered chicks.

It was such a homey place that we felt welcome and perfectly comfortable at once. The inside of the house will not be hard to describe. It was clean as could be, but with a typical bachelor's cleanliness: there was no dirt, but a great deal of disorder. Across the head of the iron bed was hung a miscellany of socks, neckties, and suspenders. A discouraging assortment of boots, shoes, and leggings protruded from beneath the bed. Some calendars ornamented the wall, and upon a table stood a smoky lamp and some tobacco and a smelly pipe. On a rack over the door lay a rifle.

Pretty soon our host came bustling in and exclaimed, "The kitchen is more pleasant than this room and there's a fire there, too." Then, catching sight of his lamp, he picked it up hurriedly and said, "Jest as shore as I leave anything undone, that shore somebody comes and sees how slouchy I am. Come on into the kitchen where you can warm, and I'll clean this lamp. One of the cows was sick this morning; I hurried over things so as to doctor her, and I forgot the lamp. I smoke and the lamp smokes to keep me company."

The kitchen would have delighted the heart of any one. Two great windows, one in the east and one in the south, gave plenty of sunlight. A shining new range and a fine assortment of vessels—which were not all yet in their place—were in one corner. There was a slow ticking clock up on a high shelf; near the door stood a homemade washstand with a tin basin, and above it hung a long narrow mirror. On the back of the door was a towel-rack. The floor was made of white pine and was spotlessly clean. In the centre of the room stood the table, with a cover of red oilcloth. Some chairs were placed about the table, but our host quickly hauled them out for us. He opened his storeroom and told us to "dish in dirty-face," and help ourselves to anything we wanted, because we were to be his "somebody come" for that night; then he hurried out to help with the teams again. He was so friendly and so likeable that we didn't feel a bit backward about "dishin' in," and it was not long before we had a smoking supper on the table.

While we were at supper he said, "I wonder, now, if any of you women can make aprons and bonnets. I don't mean them dinky little things like they make now, but rale wearin' things like they used to make."

I was afraid of another advertisement romance and didn't reply, but Mrs. O'Shaughnessy said, "Indade we can, none better."

Then he answered, "I want a blue chambray bonnet and a bunch of aprons made for my mother. She is on the way here from Pennsylvania. I ain't seen her for fifteen years. I left home longer 'n that ago, but I remember everything,—just how everything looked,—and I'd like to have things inside the house as nearly like home as I can, anyway."

I didn't know how long we could stop there, so I still made no promises, but Mrs. O'Shaughnessy could easily answer every question for a dozen women.

"Have you the cloth?" she asked.

Yes, he said; he had had it for a long time, but he had not had it sewn because he had not been sure mother *could* come.

"What's your name?" asked Mrs. O'Shaughnessy.

He hesitated a moment, then said, "Daniel Holt."

I wondered why he hesitated, but forgot all about it when Clyde said we would stop there for a few days, if we wanted to help Mr. Holt. Mrs. O'Shaughnessy's mind was already made up. Elizabeth said she would be glad to help, and I was not long in deciding when Daniel said, "I'll take it as a rale friendly favour if you women could help, because mother ain't had what could rightly be called a home since I left home. She's crippled, too, and I want to do all I can. I know she'd just like to have some aprons and a sunbonnet."

His eyes had such a pathetic, appealing look that I was ashamed, and we at once began planning our work. Daniel helped with the dishes and as soon as they were done brought out his cloth. He had a heap of it,—a bolt of checked gingham, enough blue chambray for half a dozen bonnets, and a great many remnants which he said he had bought from peddlers from time to time. Mrs. O'Shaughnessy selected what she said we would begin on, and dampened it so as to shrink it by morning. We then spread our beds and made ready for an early start next day.

Next morning we ate breakfast by the light of the lamp that smoked for the sake of companionship, and then started to cut out our work. Daniel and Mr. Stewart went fishing, and we packed their lunch so as to have them out of the way all day. I undertook the making of the bonnet, because I knew how, and because I can remember the kind my mother wore; I reckoned Daniel's mother would have worn about the same style. Mrs. O'Shaughnessy and Elizabeth can both cross-stitch, so they went out to Daniel's granary and ripped up some grain-bags, in order to get the thread with which they were sewed, to work one apron in cross-stitch.

But when we were ready to sew we were dismayed, for there was no machine. Mrs. O'Shaughnessy, however, was of the opinion that *someone* in the country must have a sewing machine, so she saddled a horse and went out, she said, to "beat the brush."

She was hardly out of sight before a man rode up and said there had been a telephone message saying that Mrs. Holt had arrived in Rock Springs, and was on her way as far as Newfork in an automobile. That threw Elizabeth and myself into a panic. We posted the messenger off on a hunt for Daniel. Elizabeth soon got over her flurry and went at her cross-stitching. I hardly knew what to do, but acting from force of habit, I reckon, I began cleaning. A powerfully good way to reason out things sometimes is to work; and just then I had to work. I began on the storeroom, which was well lighted and which was also used as a pantry.

As soon as I began straightening up I began to wonder where the mother would sleep. By arranging things in the storeroom a little differently, I was able to make room for a bed and a trunk. I decided on putting Daniel there; so then I began work in earnest. Elizabeth laid down her work and helped me. We tacked white cheesecloth over the wall, and although the floor was clean, we scrubbed it to freshen it. We polished the window until it sparkled. We were right in the middle of our work when Mrs. O'Shaughnessy came, and Daniel with her.

They were all excitement, but Mrs. O'Shaughnessy is a real general and soon marshaled her forces. Daniel had to go to Newfork after his mother; that would take three days. Mrs. O'Shaughnessy pointed out to him the need of a few pieces of furniture; so he took a wagon and team, which he got a neighbour to drive, while he took another team and a buggy for his mother. Newfork is a day's drive beyond Pinedale, and the necessary furniture could be had in Pinedale; so the neighbour went along and brought back a new bed, a rocker, and some rugs. But of course he had to stay overnight. I was for keeping right on house-cleaning; but as Mrs. O'Shaughnessy had arranged for us all to come and sew that afternoon at a near-by house, we took our sewing and clambered into the buckboard and set out.

We found Mrs. Bonham a pleasant little woman whose husband had earned her pretty new machine by chewing tobacco. I reckon you think that is a mighty funny method of earning anything, but some tobacco has tags which are redeemable, and the machine was one of the premiums. Mrs. Bonham just beamed with pride as she rolled out her machine. "I never had a machine before," she explained. "I just went to the neighbours' when I had to sew. So of course I wanted a machine awfully bad. So Frank jest chawed and chawed, and I saved every tag till we got enough, and last year we got the machine. Frank is chawin' out a clock now; but that won't take him so long as the machine did."

Well, the "chawed-out" machine did splendidly, and we turned out some good work that afternoon. I completed the blue bonnet which was to be used as "best," and made a "splint" bonnet. Mrs. O'Shaughnessy and Elizabeth did well on their aprons. We took turns about at the machine and not a minute was wasted. Mrs. Bonham showed us some crochet lace which she said she hoped to sell; and right at once Mrs. O'Shaughnessy's fertile mind begin to hatch plans. She would make Mrs. Holt a "Sunday apron," she said, and she bought the lace to trim it with. I thought Mrs. Holt must be an old-fashioned lady who liked pillow-shams. Mrs. Bonham had a pretty pair she was willing to sell. On one was worked, "Good Morning"; on the other, "Good Night"; it was done with red cotton.

The shams had a dainty edge of homemade lace. Elizabeth would not be outdone; she purchased a star quilt pieced in red and white. At sundown we went home. We were all tired, but as soon as supper was over we went to work again. We took down the bed and set it up in Dan's new quarters, and we made such headway on what had been his bedroom that we knew we could finish in a little while next day.

The next morning, as soon as we had breakfasted, Mrs. O'Shaughnessy and Elizabeth went back to sew, taking with them a lot of white cheesecloth for lining for the bedroom we were preparing for Mrs. Holt. Mr. Stewart had had fine luck fishing, but he said he felt plumb left out with so much bustling about and he not helping. He is very handy with a saw and hammer, and he contrived what we called a "chist of drawers," for Daniel's room. The "chist" had only one drawer; into that we put all the gloves, ties, handkerchiefs, and suspenders, and on the shelves below we put his shoes and boots. Then I made a blue curtain for the "chist" and one for the window, and the room looked plumb nice, I can tell you. I liked the "chist" so well that I asked Mr. Stewart to make something of the kind for Mrs. Holt's room. He said there wouldn't be time, but he went to work on it.

Promptly at noon Mrs. O'Shaughnessy and Elizabeth came with the lining for the room. We worked like beavers, and had the room sweet and ready by mid-afternoon, when the man came from Pinedale with the new furniture. In just a little while we had the room in perfect order: the bed nicely made with soft, new blankets for sheets; the pretty star quilt on, and the nice, clean pillows protected by the shams. They could buy no rugs, but a weaver of rag carpets in Pinedale had some pieces of carpet which Daniel sent back to us. They were really better and greatly more in keeping. We were very proud of the pretty white and red room when we were through. Only the kitchen was left, but we decided we could clean that early next day; so we sat down to sew and to plan the next day's dinner. We could hear Mr. Stewart out in the barn hammering and sawing on the "chist."

While we were debating whether to have fried chicken or trout for dinner, two little girls, both on one horse, rode up. They entered shyly, and after carefully explaining to us that they had heard that a wagon-load of women were buying everything they could see, had run Mr. Holt off, and were living in his house, they told us they had come to sell us some blueing. When they got two dollars' worth sold, the blueing company would send them a big doll; so, please, would we buy a lot?

We didn't think we could use any blueing, but we hated to disappoint the little things. We talked along, and presently they told us of their mother's flowers. Daniel had told us his mother *always* had a red flower in her kitchen window. When the little girls assured us their mother had a red geranium in bloom, Mrs. O'Shaughnessy set out to get it; and about dark she returned with a beautiful plant just beginning to bloom. We were all as happy as children; we had all worked very hard, too. Mr. Stewart said we deserved no sympathy because we cleaned a perfectly clean house; but, anyway, we felt much better for having gone over it.

The "chist" was finished early next morning. It would have looked better, perhaps, if it had had a little paint, but as we had no paint and were short of time, we persuaded ourselves it looked beautiful with only its clean, pretty curtain. We didn't make many changes in the kitchen. All we did was to take down the mirror and turn it lengthways above the mantel-shelf over the fireplace. We put the new rocker in the bright, sunny corner, where it would be easier for dim old eyes to see to read or sew. We set the geranium on the broad clean sill of the window, and I think you would have agreed with us that it was a cosy, cheerful home to come to after fifteen years of lonely homelessness. We couldn't get the dinner question settled, so we "dished in dirty-face"; each cooked what she thought best. Like Samantha Ann Allen, we had "everything good and plenty of it."

Elizabeth took a real interest and worked well. She is the *dearest* girl and would be a precious daughter to some mother. She has not yet told us anything about herself. All we know is, she taught school somewhere in the East. She was a little surprised at the way we took possession of a stranger's home, but she enjoyed it as much as we. "It is so nice to be doing something for some one again, something real homey and family-like," she remarked as she laid the table for dinner.

We had dinner almost ready when we heard the wheels crossing the mossy log bridge. We raced to let down the bars. Beside Daniel sat a dear dumpy little woman, her head very much bundled up with a lot of old black veils. Daniel drove through the corral, into the yard, and right up to the door. He helped her out *so* gently. She kept admonishing him, "Careful, Danyul, careful." He handed out her crutch and helped her into the kitchen, where she sank, panting, into the rocker. "It is my leg," she explained; "it has been that way ever since Danyul was a baby." Then she pleaded, "Careful, careful," to Elizabeth, who was tenderly unwrapping her. "I wouldn't have anything happen to this brown alapacky for anything; it is my very best, and I've had it ever since before I went to the pore farm; but I wanted to look nice for Danyul, comin' to his home for the first time an' all."

We had the happiest dinner party I ever remember. It would be powerfully hard for me to say which was happier, "Danyul" or his mother. They just beamed upon each other. She was proud of her boy and his pleasant home. "Danyul says he's got a little red heifer for me and he's got ten cows of his own. Now ain't that fine? It is a pity we can't have a few apple trees,—a little orchard. We'd live like kings, we would that." We explained to her how we got our fruit by parcel post, and Danyul said he would order his winter supply of apples at once.

As soon as dinner was over, Danyul had to mend a fence so as to keep his cattle in their own pasture. Mr. Stewart went to help and we women were left alone. We improved the time well. Mrs. Holt would not lie down and rest, as we tried to persuade her to, but hobbled about, admiring everything. She was delighted with the big, clean cellar and its orderly bins, in which Danyul was beginning to store his vegetables. She was as pleased as a child with her room, and almost wept when we told her which were "welcoming presents" from us. She was particularly delighted with her red flower, and Mrs. O'Shaughnessy will be happy for days remembering it was she who gave it. I shall be happy longer than that remembering how tickled she was with her bonnets.

She wanted to wipe the dishes, so she and I did up the dishes while Mrs. O'Shaughnessy and Elizabeth put some finishing stitches in on their aprons. She sat on the highest seat we could find, and as she deftly handled the dishes she told us this:—

"I should think you would wonder why Danyul ain't got me out of the porehouse before now. I've been there more 'n ten years, but Danyul didn't know it till a month ago. Charlotte Nash wrote him. Neither Danyul nor me are any master-hand at writin', and then I didn't want him to know anyhow. When Danyul got into trouble, I signed over the little farm his pa left us, to pay the lawyer person to defend him. Danyul had enough trouble, so he went to the penitentiary without finding out I was homeless. I should think you would be put out to know Danyul has been to the pen, but he has. He always said to me that he never done what he was accused of, so I am not going to tell you what it was. Danyul was always a good boy, honest and good to me and a hard worker. I ain't got no call to doubt him when he says he's innocent.

"Well, I fought his case the best I could, but he got ten years. Then the lawyer person claimed the home an' all, so I went out to work, but bein' crippled I found it hard. When Danyul had been gone four years I had saved enough to buy my brown alapacky and go to see him. He looked pale and sad,—afraid even to speak to his own mother. I went back to work as broke up as Danyul, and that winter I come down with such a long spell of sickness that they sent me to the pore farm. I always wrote to Danyul on his birthday and I couldn't bear to let him know where I was.

"Soon's his time was out, he come here; he couldn't bear the scorn that he'd get at home, so he come out to this big, free West, and took the chance it offers. Once he wrote and asked me if I would like to live West. He said if I did, after he got a start I must sell out and come to him. Bless his heart, all that time I was going to my meals just when I was told to and eatin' just what I was helped to, going to bed and getting up at some one else's word! Oh, it was bitter, but I didn't want Danyul to taste it; so, when I didn't come, he thought I didn't want to give up the old home, and didn't say no more about it. Charlotte was on the pore farm too, until her cousin died and she got left a home and enough to live on. Sometimes she would come out to the farm and take me back with her for a little visit. She was good that way. I never would tell her about Danyul; but this summer I was helpin' her dry apples and somehow she jist coaxed the secret out. She wrote to Danyul, and he wrote to me, and here I am. Danyul and me are so happy that we are goin' to send a ticket back to the farm for Maggie Harper. She ain't got no home and will be glad to help me and get a rale home."

Mrs. O'Shaughnessy and Elizabeth debated what more was needed to make the kitchen a bit more homey. Mrs. O'Shaughnessy said a red cushion for the rocker, and Elizabeth said a white cat to lie on the hearth. Mrs. Holt said, "Yes, I *do* need 'em both,—only it must be an old stray tabby cat. This house is going to be the shelter of the homeless."

Well, I can't tell you any more about the Holts because we left next morning. Danyul came across the bridge to bid us goodbye. He said he could never thank us enough, but it is we who should be and are thankful. We got a little glow of happiness from their great blaze. We are all so glad to know that everything is secure and bright for the Holts in the future.

That stop is the cause of my missing two letters to you, but this letter is as long as half a dozen letters should be. You know I never could get along with few words. I'll try to do better next time. But I can't imagine how I shall get the letters mailed. We are miles and miles and miles away in the mountains; it is two days' ride to a post-office, so maybe I will not get letters to you as often as I planned.

Sincerely yours,

Elinore Rupert Stewart.

6

Elizabeth's Romance

Dear Mrs. Coney,—

I find I can't write to you as often as I at first intended; but I've a chance today, so I will not let it pass unused. We are in the last camp, right on the hunting ground, in the "midst of the fray." We have said goodbye to dear Elizabeth, and I must tell you about her because she really comes first.

To begin with, the morning we left the Holts, Elizabeth suggested that we three women ride in the buckboard, so I seated myself on a roll of bedding in the back part. At first none of us talked; we just absorbed the wonderful green-gold beauty of the morning. The sky was clear blue, with a few fleecy clouds drifting lazily past. The mountains on one side were crested; great crags and piles of rock crowned them as far as we could see; timber grew only about halfway up. The trunks of the quaking aspens shone silvery in the early sunlight, and their leaves were shimmering gold. And the stately pines kept whispering and murmuring; it almost seemed as if they were chiding the quaking aspens for being frivolous. On the other side of the road lay the river, bordered by willows and grassy flats. There were many small lakes, and the ducks and geese were noisily enjoying themselves among the rushes and water-grasses. Beyond the river rose the forest-covered mountains, hill upon hill.

Elizabeth dressed with especial care that morning, and very pretty she looked in her neat shepherd's plaid suit and natty little white canvas hat. Very soon she said, "I hope neither of you will misunderstand me when I tell you that if my hopes are realized I will not ride with you much longer. I never saw such a country as the West,—it is so big

171

and so beautiful,—and I never saw such people. You are just like your country; you have fed me, cared for me, and befriended me, a stranger, and never asked me a word."

Mrs. O'Shaughnessy said, "Tut, tut, 'tis nothing at all we've done. 'Tis a comfort you've been, hasn't she, Mrs. Stewart?"

I could heartily agree; and Elizabeth went on, "The way I have been received and the way we all treated Mrs. Holt will be the greatest help to me in becoming what I hope to become, a real Westerner. I might have lived a long time in the West and not have understood many things if I had not fallen into your hands. Years ago, before I was through school, I was to have been married; but I lost my mother just then and was left the care of my paralytic father. If I had married then, I should have had to take father from his familiar surroundings, because Wallace came West in the forestry service. I felt that it wouldn't be right. Poor father couldn't speak, but his eyes told me how grateful he was to stay. We had our little home and father had his pension, and I was able to get a small school near us. I could take care of father and teach also. We were very comfortably situated, and in time became really happy. Although I seldom heard from Wallace, his letters were well worth waiting for, and I knew he was doing well.

"Eighteen months ago father died,—gently went to sleep. I waited six months and then wrote to Wallace, but received no reply. I have written him three times and have had no word. I could bear it no longer and have come to see what has become of him. If he is dead, may I stay on with one of you and perhaps get a school? I want to live here always."

"But, darlint," said Mrs. O'Shaughnessy, "supposin' it's married your man is?"

"Wallace may have changed his mind about me, but he would not marry without telling me. If he is alive he is honourable."

Then I asked, "Why didn't you ask about him at Pinedale or any of these places we have passed? If he is stationed in the Bridges reserve they would be sure to know of him at any of these little places."

"I just didn't have the courage to. I should never have told you what I have, only I think I owe it to you, and it was easier because of the Holts. I am so glad we met them."

So we drove along, talking together; we each assured the girl of our entire willingness to have her as a member of the family. After a while I got on to the wagon with Mr. Stewart and told him Elizabeth's story so that he could inquire about the man. Soon we came to the crossing on Green River. Just beyond the ford we could see the game-warden's cabin, with the stars and stripes fluttering gayly in the fresh morning breeze. We drove into the roaring, dashing water, and we held our breath until we emerged on the other side.

Mr. Sorenson is a very capable and conscientious game-warden and a very genial gentleman. He rode down to meet us, to inspect our license and to tell us about our privileges and our duties as good woodsmen. He also issues licenses in case hunters have neglected to secure them before coming. Mrs. O'Shaughnessy had refused to get a license when we did. She said she was not going to hunt; she told us we could give her a small piece of "ilk" and that would do; so we were rather surprised when she purchased two licenses, one a special, which would entitle her to a bull elk. As we were starting Mr. Stewart asked the game-warden, "Can you tell me if Wallace White is still stationed here?"

"Oh, yes," Mr. Sorenson said, "Wallace's place is only a few miles up the river and can be plainly seen from the road."

We drove on. Happiness had taken a new clutch upon my heart. I looked back, expecting to see Elizabeth all smiles, but if you will believe me the foolish girl was sobbing as if her heart was broken. Mrs. O'Shaughnessy drew her head down upon her shoulder and was trying to quiet her. The road along there was *very* rough. Staying on the wagon occupied all my attention for a while. Several miles were passed when we came in sight of a beautiful cabin, half hidden in a grove of pines beyond the river. Mr. Stewart said we might as well "noon" as soon as we came to a good place, and then he would ride across and see Mr. White.

Just as we rounded the hill a horseman came toward us. A splendid fellow he was, manly strength and grace showing in every line. The road was narrow against the hillside and he had to ride quite close, so I saw his handsome face plainly. As soon as he saw Elizabeth he sprang from his saddle and said, "'Liz'beth, 'Liz'beth, what you doin' here?"

She held her hands to him and said, "Oh, just riding with friends." Then to Mrs. O'Shaughnessy she said, "*This* is my Wallace."

Mr. Stewart is the queerest man: instead of letting me enjoy the tableau, he solemnly drove on, saying he would not want anyone gawking at him if he were the happy man. Anyway, he couldn't urge Chub fast enough to prevent my seeing and hearing what I've told you. Besides that, I saw that Elizabeth's hat was on awry, her hair in disorder, and her eyes red. It was disappointing after she had been so careful to look nicely.

Mrs. O'Shaughnessy came trotting along and we stopped for dinner. We had just got the coffee boiling when the lovers came up, Elizabeth in the saddle, "learning to ride," and he walking beside her holding her hand. How happy they were! The rest of us were mighty near as foolish as they. They were going to start immediately after dinner, on horseback, for the county seat, to be married. After we had eaten, Elizabeth selected a few things from her trunk, and Mr. Stewart and Mr. White drove the buckboard across the river to leave the trunk in its new home. While they were gone we helped Elizabeth to dress. All the while Mrs. O'Shaughnessy was admonishing her to name her first "girul" Mary Ellen; "or," she said, "if yer first girul happens to be a b'y, it's Sheridan ye'll be callin' him, which was me name before I was married to me man, God rest his soul."

Dear Elizabeth, she was glad to get away, I suspect! She and her Wallace made a fine couple as they rode away in the golden September afternoon. I believe she is *one* happy bride that the sun shone on, if the omen has failed *everywhere* else.

Well, we felt powerfully reduced in numbers, but about three o'clock that afternoon we came upon Mr. Struble and Mr. Haynes waiting beside the road for us. They had come to pilot us into camp, for there would be no road soon.

Such a way as we came over! Such jolting and sliding! I begged to get off and walk; but as the whole way was carpeted by strawberry vines and there were late berries to tempt me to loiter, I had to stay on the wagon. I had no idea a wagon could be got across such places.

Mr. Struble drove for Mrs. O'Shaughnessy, and I could hear her imploring all the saints to preserve us from instant death. I kept shutting my eyes, trying not to see the terrifying places, and opening them again to see the beauty spread everywhere, until Mr. Stewart said, "It must make you nervous to ride over mountain roads. Don't bat your eyes so fast and you'll see more." So then I stiffened my back and kept my eyes open, and I *did* see more.

It had been decided to go as far as we could with the wagons and then set camp; from there the hunters would ride horseback as far up as they could and then climb. It was almost sundown when we reached camp. All the hunters were in, and such a yowling as they set up! "Look who's here! See who's come!" they yelled. They went to work setting up tents and unloading wagons with a hearty good-will.

We are camped just on the edge of the pines. Back of us rises a big pine-clad mountain; our tents are set under some big trees, on a small plateau, and right below us is a valley in which grass grows knee high and little streams come from every way. Trout scurry up stream whenever we go near. We call the valley Paradise Valley because it is the horses' paradise. And as in the early morning we can often see clouds rolling along the valley, we call our camp Cloudcrest. We have a beautiful place: it is well sheltered; there is plenty of wood, water, and feed; and, looking eastward down the valley, snow-covered, crag-topped mountains delight the eye.

The air is so bracing that we all feel equal to *anything*. Mr. Struble has already killed a fine "spike" elk for camp eating. We camped in a bunch, and we have camp stoves so that in case of rain or snow we can stay indoors. Just now we have a huge camp fire around which we sit in the evening, telling stories, singing, and eating nuts of the *piñon* pine. Then too the whole country is filled with those tiny little strawberries. We have to gather all day to get as much as we can eat, but they are delicious. Yesterday we had pie made of wild currants; there are a powerful lot of them here. There is also a little blueberry that the men say is the Rocky Mountain huckleberry. The grouse are feeding on them. Altogether this is one of the most delightful places imaginable. The men are not very anxious to begin hunting. A little delay means cooler weather for the meat. It is cool up here, but going back across the desert it will be warm for a while yet. Still, when they see elk every day it is a great temptation to try a shot.

One of the students told me Professor Glenholdt was here to get the tip-end bone of the tail of a brontosaurus. I don't know what that is, but if it is a fossil he won't get it, for the soil is too deep. The students are jolly, likable fellows, but they can talk of nothing but *strata* and formation. I heard one of them say he would be glad when some one killed a bear, as he had heard they were fine eating, having *strata* of fat alternating with *strata* of lean. Mr. Haynes is a quiet fellow, just interested in hunting. Mr. Struble is the big man of the party; he is tall and strong and we find him very pleasant company. Then there is Dr. Teschall; he is a quiet fellow with an unexpected smile. He is so reserved that I felt that he was kind of out of place among the rest until I caught his cordial smile. He is so slight that I don't see how he will stand the hard climbing, not to mention carrying the heavy gun. They are using the largest calibre sporting guns,—murderous-looking things. That is, all except Mr. Harkrudder, the picture man. He looks to be about forty years old, but whoops and laughs like he was about ten.

I don't need to tell you of the "good mon," do I? He is just the kind, quiet good mon that he has always been since I have known him. A young lady from a neighbouring camp came over and said she had called to see our *tout ensemble*. Well, I've given you it, they, us, or we.

We didn't need a guide, as Mr. Haynes and Mr. Struble are old-timers. We were to have had a cook, but when we reached Pinedale, where we were to have picked him up, he told Mr. Haynes he was "too tam seek in de bel," so we had to come without him; but that is really no inconvenience, since we are all very good cooks and are all willing to help. I don't think I shall be able to tell you of any great exploits I make with the gun. I fired one that Mr. Stewart carries, and it almost kicked my shoulder off. I am mystified about Mrs. O'Shaughnessy's license. I know she would not shoot one of those big guns for a dozen elk; besides that, she is very tender-hearted and will never harm anything herself, although she likes to join our hunts.

I think you must be tired of this letter, so I am going to say good-night, my friend.

E. R. S.

7

The Hunt

Dear Mrs. Coney,—

It seems so odd to be writing you and getting no answers. Mrs. O'Shaughnessy just now asked me what I have against you that I write you so much. I haven't one thing. I told her I owed you more love than I could ever pay in a lifetime, and she said writing such *long* letters is a mighty poor way to show it. I have been neglecting you shamefully, I think. One of the main reasons I came on this hunt was to take the trip for *you*, and to tell you things that you would most enjoy. So I will spend this snowy day in writing to you.

On the night of September 30, there was the most awful thunderstorm I ever witnessed,—flash after flash of the most blinding lightning, followed by deafening peals of thunder; and as it echoed from mountain to mountain the uproar was terrifying. I have always loved a storm; the beat of hail and rain, and the roar of wind always appeal to me; but there was neither wind nor rain,—just flash and roar. Before the echo died away among the hills another booming report would seem to shiver the atmosphere and set all our tinware jangling. We are camped so near the great pines that I will confess I was powerfully afraid. Had the lightning struck one of the big pines there would not have been one of us left. I could hear Mrs. O'Shaughnessy murmuring her prayers when there was a lull.

We had gone to bed, but I couldn't remain there; so I sat on the wagon-seat with Jerrine beside me. Something struck the guy ropes of the tent, and I was so frightened I was too weak to cry out. I thought the big tree must have fallen. In the lulls of the storm I could hear the men's voices, high and excited. They, too, were up. It seemed to me that the storm lasted for hours; but at last it moved off up the valley, the flashes grew to be a mere glimmer, and the thunder mere rumbling. The pines began to moan, and soon a little breeze whistled by. So we lay down again. Next morning the horses could not be found; the storm had frightened them, and they had tried to go home. The men had to find them, and as it took most of the day, we had to put off our hunt.

We were up and about next morning in the first faint gray light. While the men fed grain to the horses and saddled them, we prepared a hasty breakfast. We were off before it was more than light enough for us to see the trail.

Dawn in the mountains—how I wish I could describe it to you! If I could only make you feel the keen, bracing air, the exhilarating climb; if I could only paint its beauties, what a picture you should have! Here the colours are very different from those of the desert. I suppose the forest makes it so. The shadows are mellow, like the colours in an old picture—greenish amber light and a blue-gray sky. Far ahead of us we could see the red rim rock of a mountain above timber line. The first rays of the sun turned the jagged peaks into golden points of a crown. In Oklahoma, at that hour of the day, the woods would be alive with song-birds, even at this season; but here there are no song-birds, and only the snapping of twigs, as our horses climbed the frosty trail, broke the silence. We had been cautioned not to talk, but neither Mrs. O'Shaughnessy nor I wanted to. Afterwards, when we compared notes, we found that we both had the same thought: we both felt ashamed to be out to deal death to one of the Maker's beautiful creatures, and we were planning how we might avoid it.

The sun was well up when we reached the little park where we picketed our horses. Then came a long, hard climb. It is hard climbing at the best, and when there is a big gun to carry, it is *very* hard. Then too, we had to keep up with the men, and we didn't find that easy to do. At last we reached the top and sat down on some boulders to rest a few minutes before we started down to the hunting ground, which lay in a cuplike valley far below us.

We could hear the roar of the Gros Ventre as it tumbled grumblingly over its rocky bed. To our right rose mile after mile of red cliffs. As the last of the quaking asp leaves have fallen, there were no golden groves. In their places stood silvery patches against the red background of the cliffs. High overhead a triangle of wild geese harrowed the blue sky.

I was plumb out of breath, but men who are most gallant else-where are absolutely heartless on a hunt. I was scarcely through pant-ing before we began to descend. We received instructions as to how we should move so as to keep out of range of each other's guns; then Mr. Haynes and myself started one way, and Mr. Struble and Mrs. O'Shaughnessy the other. We were to meet where the valley termi-nated in a broad pass. We felt sure we could get a chance at what elk there might be in the valley. We were following fresh tracks, and a little of the hunter's enthusiasm seized me.

We had not followed them far when three cows and a "spike" came running out of the pines a little ahead of us. Instantly Mr. Hay-nes's gun flew to his shoulder and a deafening report jarred our ears. He ran forward, but I stood still, fascinated by what I saw. Our side of the valley was bounded by a rim of rock. Over the rim was a sheer wall of rock for two hundred feet, to where the Gros Ventre was an-grily roaring below; on the other side of the stream rose the red cliffs with their jagged crags. At the report of the gun two huge blocks of stone almost as large as a house detached themselves and fell. At the same instant one of the quaking asp groves began to move slowly. I couldn't believe my eyes. I shut them a moment, but when I looked the grove was moving faster. It slid swiftly, and I could plainly hear the rattle of stones falling against stones, until with a muffled roar the whole hillside fell into the stream.

Mr. Haynes came running back. "What is the matter? Are you hurt? Why didn't you shoot?" he asked.

I waved my hand weakly toward where the great mound of tan-gled trees and earth blocked the water. "Why," he said, "that is only a landslide, not an earthquake. You are as white as a ghost. Come on up here and see my fine elk."

I sat on a log watching him dress his elk. We have found it best not to remove the skin, but the elk have to be quartered so as to load them on to a horse. Mrs. O'Shaughnessy and Mr. Struble came out of the woods just then. They had seen a big bunch of elk headed by a splendid bull, but got no shot, and the elk went out of the pass. They had heard our shot, and came across to see what luck.

"What iver is the matter with ye?" asked Mrs. O'Shaughnessy. Mr. Haynes told her. They had heard the noise, but had thought it thunder. Mr. Haynes told me that if I would "chirk up" he would give me his elk teeth. Though I don't admire them, they are considered valuable; however, his elk was a cow, and they don't have as nice teeth as do bulls.

We had lunch, and the men covered the elk with pine boughs to keep the camp robbers from pecking it full of holes. Next day the men would come with the horses and pack it in to camp. We all felt refreshed; so we started on the trail of those that got away.

For a while walking was easy and we made pretty good time; then we had a rocky hill to get over. We had to use care when we got into the timber; there were marshy places which tried us sorely, and windfall so thick that we could hardly get through. We were obliged to pick our way carefully to avoid noise, and we were all together, not having come to a place where it seemed better to separate. We had about resolved to go to our horses when we heard a volley of shots.

"That is somebody bunch-shooting," said Mr. Struble. "They are in Brewster Lake Park, by the sound. That means that the elk will pass here in a short time and we may get a shot. The elk will be here long before the men, since the men have no horses; so let's hurry and get placed along the only place they can get out. We'll get our limit."

We hastily secreted ourselves along the narrow gorge through which the elk must pass. We were all on one side, and Mr. Haynes said to me, "Rest your gun on that rock and aim at the first rib back of the shoulder. If you shoot haphazard you may cripple an elk and let it get away to die in misery. So make sure when you fire."

It didn't seem a minute before we heard the beat of their hoofs and a queer panting noise that I can't describe. First came a beautiful thing with his head held high; his great antlers seemed to lie half his length on his back; his eyes were startled, and his shining black mane seemed to bristle. I heard the report of guns, and he tumbled in a confused heap. He tried to rise, but others coming leaped over him and knocked him down. Some more shots, and those behind turned and went back the way they had come.

Mr. Haynes shouted to me, "Shoot, shoot; why *don't* you shoot!"

So I fired my Krag, but next I found myself picking myself up and wondering who had struck me and for what. I was so dizzy I could scarcely move, but I got down to where the others were excitedly admiring the two dead elk that they said were the victims of Mrs. O'Shaughnessy's gun. She was as excited and delighted as if she had never declared she would not kill anything. "Sure, it's many a meal they'll make for little hungry mouths," she said. She was rubbing her shoulder ruefully. "I don't want to fire any more big guns. I thought old Goliar had hit me a biff with a blackthorn shilaley," she remarked.

Mr. Haynes turned to me and said, "You are a dandy hunter! you didn't shoot at all until after the elk were gone, and the way you held your gun it is a wonder it didn't knock your head off, instead of just smashing your jaw."

The men worked as fast as they could at the elk, and we helped as much as we could, but it was dark before we reached camp. Supper was ready, but I went to bed at once. They all thought it was because I was so disappointed, but it was because I was so stiff and sore I could hardly move, and so tired I couldn't sleep. Next morning my jaw and neck were so swollen that I hated anyone to see me, and my head ached for two days. It has been snowing for a long time, but Clyde says he will take me hunting when it stops. I don't want to go but reckon I will have to, because I don't want to come so far and buy a license to kill an elk and go back empty-handed, and partly to get a rest from Mr. Murry's everlasting accordion.

Mr. Murry is an old-time acquaintance of Mrs. O'Shaughnessy's. He has a ranch down on the river somewhere. Mrs. O'Shaughnessy has not seen him for years,—didn't know he lived up here. He had seen the game-warden from whom she had procured her license, and so hunted up our camp. He is an odd-looking individual, with sad eyes and a drooping mouth which gives his face a most hopeless, reproachful expression. His nose, however, seems to upset the original plan, for it is long and thin and bent slightly to one side. His neck is long and his Adam's apple seems uncertain as to where it belongs. At supper Jerrine watched it as if fascinated until I sent her from the table and went out to speak to her about gazing.

"Why, mamma," she said, "I had to look; he has swallowed something that won't go either up or down, and I'm 'fraid he'll choke."

Although I can't brag about Mr. Murry's appearance, I can about his taste, for he admires Mrs. O'Shaughnessy. It seems that in years gone by he has made attempts to marry her.

As he got up from supper the first night he was with us, he said, "Mary Ellen, I have a real treat and surprise for you. Just wait a few minutes, an' I'll bet you'll be happy."

We took our accustomed places around the fire, while Mr. Murry hobbled his *cayuse* and took an odd-looking bundle from his saddle. He seated himself and took from the bundle—an accordion! He set it upon his knee and began pulling and pushing on it. He did what Mr. Struble said was doling a doleful tune. Everyone took it good-

181

naturedly, but he kept doling the doleful until little by little the circle thinned.

Our tent is as comfortable as can be. Now that it is snowing, we sit around the stoves, and we should have fine times if Professor Glenholdt could have a chance to talk; but we have to listen to "Run, Nigger, Run" and "The Old Gray Hoss Come A-tearin' Out The Wilderness." I'll sing them to you when I come to Denver.

With much love to you,

Elinore Rupert Stewart.

8

The Seventh Man

Cloudcrest, October 10, 1914.

Dear Mrs. Coney,—

I wonder what you would do if you were here. But I reckon I had better not anticipate, and so I will begin at the beginning. On the morning of the eighth we held a council. The physician and the two students had gone. All had their limit of elk except Mr. Haynes and myself. Our licenses also entitled each of us to a deer, a mountain sheep, and a bear. We had plenty of food, but it had snowed about a foot and I was beginning to want to get out while the going was good. Two other outfits had gone out. The doctor and the students hired them to haul out their game. So we decided to stay on a week longer.

That morning Mrs. O'Shaughnessy and I melted snow and washed the clothes. It was delightful to have nice soft water, and we enjoyed our work; it was almost noon before we thought to begin dinner. I suppose you would say lunch, but with us it is dinner. None of the men had gone out that day.

Mr. Harkrudder was busy with his films and didn't come with the rest when dinner was ready. When he did come, he was excited; he laid a picture on the table and said, "Do any of you recognise this?"

It looked like a flashlight of our camping ground. It was a little blurry, but some of the objects were quite clear. Our tent was a white blotch except for the outlines; the wagons showed plainly. I didn't think much of it as a picture, so I paid scant attention. Mrs. O'Shaughnessy gave it close scrutiny; presently she said, "Oh, yis, I see what it is. It's a puzzle picture and ye find the man. Here he is, hidin' beyont the pine next the tent."

"Exactly," said Harkrudder, "but I had not expected just this. I am working out some ideas of my own in photography, and this picture is one of the experiments I tried the night of the storm. The result doesn't prove my experiment either way. Where were you, Stewart, during the storm?"

"Where should I be? I bided i' the bed," the Stewart said.

"Well," said Harkrudder, "I know where each of the other fellows was, and none of them was in this direction. Now who is the seventh man?"

I looked again, and, sure enough, there was a man in a crouching position outlined against the tent wall. We were all excited, for it was ten minutes past one when Harkrudder was out, and we couldn't think why anyone would be prowling about our camp at that time of the night.

As Mr. Stewart and I had planned a long, beautiful ride, we set out after dinner, leaving the rest yet at the table eating and conjecturing about the "stranger within our picture." I had hoped we would come to ground level enough for a sharp, invigorating canter, but our way was too rough. It was a joy to be out in the great, silent forest. The snow made riding a little venturesome because the horses slipped a great deal, but Chub is dependable even though he is lazy. Clyde bestrode Mr. Haynes's Old Blue. We were headed for the cascades on Clear Creek, to see the wonderful ice-caverns that the flying spray is forming.

We had almost reached the cascades and were crossing a little bowl-like valley, when an elk calf leaped out of the snow and ran a few yards. It paused and finally came irresolutely back toward us. A few steps farther we saw great, red splotches on the snow and the body of a cow elk. Around it were the tracks of the faithful little calf. It would stay by its mother until starvation or wild animals put an end to its suffering. The cow was shot in half a dozen places, none of them in a fatal spot; it had bled to death. "That," said Mr. Stewart angrily, "comes o' bunch shooting. The authorities should revoke the license of a man found guilty of bunch shooting."

We rode on in silence, each a little saddened by what we had seen. But this was not all. We had begun to descend the mountain side to Clear Creek when we came upon the beaten trail of a herd of elk. We followed it as offering perhaps the safest descent. It didn't take us far. Around the spur of the mountain the herd had stampeded; tracks were everywhere. Lying in the trail were a spike and an old bull with a broken antler. Chub shied, but Old Blue doesn't scare, so Mr. Stewart rode up quite close. Around the heads were tell-tale tracks. We didn't dismount, but we knew that the two upper teeth or tushes were missing and that the hated tooth-hunter was at work. The tracks in the snow showed there had been two men. An adult elk averages five hundred pounds of splendid meat; here before us, therefore, lay a thousand pounds of food thrown to waste just to enable a contemptible tooth-hunter to obtain four teeth. Tooth-hunting is against the law, but this is a case where you must catch before hanging.

Well, we saw the cascades, and after resting a little, we started homeward through the heavy woods, where we were compelled to go more slowly. We had dismounted, and were gathering some *piñon* cones from a fallen tree, when, almost without a sound, a band of elk came trailing down a little draw where a spring trickled. We watched them file along, evidently making for lower ground on which to bed. Chub snorted, and a large cow stopped and looked curiously in our direction. Those behind passed leisurely around her. We knew she had no calf, because she was light in colour: cows suckling calves are of a darker shade. A loud report seemed to rend the forest, and the beauty dropped. The rest disappeared so suddenly that if the fine specimen that lay before me had not been proof, it would almost have seemed a dream. I had shot the cow elk my license called for.

We took off the head and removed the entrails, then covered our game with pine boughs, to which we tied a red bandanna so as to make it easy to find next day, when the men would come back with a saw to divide it down the back and pack it in. There is an imposing row of game hanging in the pines back of our tent. Supper was ready when we got in. Mr. Haynes had been out also and was very joyful; he got his elk this afternoon. We can start home day after tomorrow. It will take the men all tomorrow to get in the game.

I shall be glad to start. I am getting homesick, and I have not had a letter or even a card since I have been here. We are hungry for war news, and besides, it is snowing again. Our clothes didn't get dry either; they are frozen to the bush we hung them on. Perhaps they will be snowed under by morning. I can't complain, though, for it is warm and pleasant in our tent. The little camp-stove is glowing. Mrs. O'Shaughnessy is showing Jerrine how to make pigs of potatoes. Calvin and Robert are asleep. The men have all gone to the bachelors' tent to form their plans, all save Mr. Murry, who is "serenading" Mrs. O'Shaughnessy. He is playing "Nelly Gray," and somehow I don't want to laugh at him as I usually do; I can only feel sorry for him.

I can hardly write because my heart is yearning for my little Junior boy at home on the ranch with his grandmother. Dear little Mother Stewart, I feel very tender toward her. Junior is the pride of her heart. She would not allow us to bring him on this trip, so she is at the ranch taking care of my brown-eyed boy. Every one is so good, so kind, and I can do so little to repay. It makes me feel very unworthy. You'll think I have the blues, but I haven't. I just feel humble and chastened. When Mr. Murry pauses I can hear the soft spat, spat of the falling snow on the tent. I will be powerfully glad when we set our faces homeward.

Goodnight, dear friend. Angels guard you.

Elinore Stewart.

9

An Indian Camp

Dear, Dear Mrs. Coney,—

This is the very last letter you will receive dated from this camp. We are leaving a few days earlier than we intended and I am pretty badly on the fence. I want to laugh, and really I can hardly keep back the tears. We are leaving sooner than we meant, for rather a good reason. We haven't one bite to eat except elk meat.

After the men had brought into camp the elk we killed the other afternoon, they began to plan a sheep hunt. As sheep do not stay in the woods, the men had to go miles away and above timber line. They decided to take a pack horse and stay all night. I didn't want Mr. Stewart to go because the climbing is very dangerous. No accidents have happened this year, but last season a man fell from the crags and was killed; so I tried to keep the "good mon" at home. But he would not be persuaded. The love of chase has entered his blood, and it looks to me as if it had chased reason plumb out of his head. I know exactly how Samantha felt when Josiah *would* go to the "pleasure exertion." The bald spot on the Stewart's head doesn't seem to remind him of years gone by; he is as joyous as a boy.

It was finally decided to take Mrs. O'Shaughnessy and the children and myself to a neighbouring camp about two miles away, as we didn't like to risk being frightened by a possible intruder. Sorenson, the game-warden, was in camp to inspect our game on the 12th, and he told us he was on the trail of tooth-hunters and had routed them out on the night of the storm; but what they could have been doing in our camp was as much a mystery to him as to us.

Well, when we were ready to go, Mr. Murry and the Stewart escorted us. It was a cloudy afternoon and often great flakes of snow fell gently, softly. The snow was already about eighteen inches deep, and it made sheep hunting slippery and dangerous work. On our way we came upon an Indian camp. They were all huddled about a tiny fire; scattered about were their *wikiups* made of sticks and pine boughs. The Indians were sullen and angry. The game-warden had ordered them back to Fort Washakie, where they belonged. Their squaws had jerked their elk. You may not know what jerked means, so I will explain: it means dried, cured. They had all they were allowed, but for some reason they didn't want to go. Sorenson suspects them of being in with the tooth-hunters and he is narrowing the circle.

At the camp where we were to stay, we found Mrs. Kavanaugh laid up with a sore throat, but she made us welcome. It would be a mighty funny camper who wouldn't. As soon as the men from the Kavanaugh camp heard our men's plans, they were eager to go along. So it ended in us three women being left alone. We said we were not afraid and we tried not to feel so, but after dark we all felt a little timorous. Mrs. Kavanaugh was afraid of the Indians, but I was afraid they would bring Clyde back dead from a fall. We were camped in an old cabin built by the ranger. The Kavanaughs were short of groceries. We cooked our big elk steaks on sticks before an open fire, and we roasted potatoes in the ashes. When our fear wore away, we had a fine time. After a while we lay down on fragrant beds of pine.

We awoke late. The fire was dead upon the hearth and outside the snow was piling up. Mrs. O'Shaughnessy made a rousing fire and managed to jolly us until we had a really happy breakfast hour. About three in the afternoon all the men came trooping in, cold, wet, and hungry. After filling them with venison, hot potatoes, and coffee, we started to our own camp. The men were rather depressed because they had come back empty-handed. The Indians were gone and the snow lay thick over the place where their fire had been; they had left in the night.

When we came to camp, Mr. Struble started to build a fire; but no matches were to be had. Next, the men went to feed grain to their tired horses, but the oats were gone. Mr. Murry sought in vain for his beloved accordion. Mr. Harkrudder was furious when he found his grinding machine was gone. Mrs. O'Shaughnessy made a dash for the grub-box. It was empty. We were dumbfounded. Each of us kept searching and researching and knowing all the while we would find nothing. Mr. Struble is a most cheerful individual, and, as Mrs. O'Shaughnessy says, "is a mighty good fellow even if he *is* Dutch."

"The Indians have stolen us out," he said, "but after all they have left us our tents and harness, all our meat, and the road home; so what matter if we *are* a little inconvenienced as to grub? Haynes may cry for sugar, but that won't hurt the rest any. I'll saddle and ride over to Scotty's and get enough to last us out."

We knew the Kavanaughs could not help us any, but we grew cheerful in anticipating help from Scotty, who was from Green River and was camped a few miles away. We wanted Mr. Struble to wait until morning, but he said no, it would make breakfast late; so he rode off in the dark. At two o'clock this morning he came in almost frozen, with two small cans of milk and two yeast cakes. As soon as it was light enough to see, the men were at work loading the game and breaking camp. As they are ready now to take down this tent, I will have to finish this letter somewhere else.

10

The Tooth-Hunters

At Sorenson's Cabin
on Green River.

Well, we're here, warmed and fed and in much better trim bodily and mentally. We had mishap after mishap coming. First the Hutton horse, being a bronco, had to act up when he was hitched up. We had almost more game than we could haul, but at last we got started, after the bronco had reared and pitched as much as he wanted to. There are a great many springs,—one every few feet in these mountains,—and the snow hid the pitfalls and made the ground soft, so that the wheels cut in and pulling was hard. Then, too, our horses had had nothing to eat for two days, the snow being so deep they couldn't get at the grass, hobbled as they were.

We had got perhaps a mile from camp when the leading wagon, with four horses driven by Mr. Haynes, suddenly stopped. The wheels had sunk into the soft banks of a small, ditch-like spring branch. Mr. Stewart had to stay on our wagon to hold the bronco, but all the rest, even Mrs. O'Shaughnessy, gathered around and tried to help. They hitched on a snap team, but not a trace tightened. They didn't want to unload the game in the snow. The men lifted and pried on the wheels. Still the horses wouldn't budge.

Mr. Haynes is no disciple of Job, but he tried manfully to restrain himself. Turning to Glenholdt, who was offering advice, he said, "You get out. I know what the trouble is: these horses used to belong to a freighter and are used to being cussed. It's the greatest nuisance in the world for a man to go out where there's a bunch of women. If these women weren't along I'd make these horses get out of there."

Mrs. O'Shaughnessy said, "Don't lay your poor driving to the women. If you drive by cussin', then *cuss*. We will stop up our ears."

She threw her apron over her head. I held my fingers in Jerrine's ears, and she stopped my ears, else I might be able to tell you what he said. It was something violent, I know. I could tell by the expression of his face. He had only been doing it a second when those horses walked right out with the wagon as nicely as you please. Mrs. O'Shaughnessy said to Mr. Haynes, "It's a poor cusser you are. Sure, it's no wonder you hesitated to begin. If Danny O'Shaughnessy couldn't have sworn better, I'd have had to hilp him."

We got along pretty well after that. Mr. Haynes kept some distance ahead; but occasionally a bit of "cussin'" came back to us and we knew he was using freighter tactics.

The game-warden lives in a tiny little cabin. The door is so low that I had to stoop to get in. It was quite dark when we got here last night, but Mrs. Sorenson acted as if she was *glad* to see us. I didn't think we could all get in. A row of bunks is built along one side of the cabin. A long tarpaulin covers the bed, and we all got upon this and sat while our hostess prepared our supper. If one of us had stirred we would have been in her way; so there we sat as thick as thieves. When supper was ready six got off their perch and ate; when they were through, six more were made happy.

Mr. Sorenson had caught the tooth-hunters. On the wall hung their deadly guns, with silencers on them to muffle the report. He showed us the teeth he had found in their possession. The warden and his deputy had searched the men and their effects and found no teeth. He had no evidence against them except their unlawful guns, but he knew he had the right men. At last he found their contract to furnish two hundred pair of teeth. It is a trick of such hunters to thrust a knife into the meat of the game they have, and so to make pockets in which they hide the teeth; but these fellows had no such pockets. They jeered at the warden and threatened to kill him, but he kept searching, and presently found the teeth in a pail of lard. He told us all about it as we sat, an eager crowd, on his bed. A warden takes his life in his hands when he goes after such fellows, but Sorenson is not afraid to do it.

The cabin walls are covered with pen-and-ink drawings, the work of the warden's gifted children,—Vina, the pretty eighteen-year-old daughter, and Laurence, the sixteen-year-old son. They never had a lesson in drawing in their lives, but their pictures portray Western life exactly.

The snow is not so deep here as it was at camp, but it is too deep for the horses to get grass. The men were able to get a little grain from the warden; so we will pull out in the morning and try to make it to where we can get groceries. We are quite close to where Elizabeth lives, but we should have to cross the river, and it was dark before we passed her home. I should like to see her but won't get a chance to. Mrs. Sorenson says she is very happy. In all this round of exposure the kiddies are as well as can be. Cold, camping, and elk meat agree with them. We are in a tent for the night, and it is so cold the ink is freezing, but the kiddies are snuggled under their blankets as warm as toast. We are to start early in the morning. Goodnight, dear friend. I am glad I can take this trip *for* you. You'd freeze.

Elinore Stewart.

11

Buddy and Baby Girl

Dear Mrs. Coney,—

The day we left the game-warden's was damp and lowering. It didn't seem it could have one good thing to its credit, but there were several things to be thankful for. One of them was that you were safe at home in your warm, dry apartment. We had hardly passed the great Block buttes when the biggest, wettest flakes of snow began to pelt into our faces. I really like a storm, and the kiddies would have enjoyed the snow; but we had to keep the wagon-sheet tied down to keep the bedding dry, and the kiddies get sick under cover. All the pleasure I might have had was taken away by the fact that we were making a forced drive. We *had* to go. The game-warden had no more than enough food for his family, and no horse feed. Also, the snow was almost as deep there as it had been higher up, so the horses could not graze.

We made it to Cora that day. Here at last was plenty of hay and grain; we restocked our mess-boxes and felt better toward the world. Next day we came on here to Newfork, where we are resting our teams before we start across the desert, which begins just across the creek we are camped on.

We have added two to our party. I know you will be interested to know how it happened, and I can picture the astonishment of our neighbours when we reach home, for our newcomers are to be members of Mrs. O'Shaughnessy's family. We had all been sorry we could not visit Elizabeth or "Danyul" and his mother. We felt almost as if we were sneaking past them, but we consoled ourselves with promises to see the Burneys and Grandma Mortimer. Yesterday the children and I were riding with Mrs. O'Shaughnessy in the buckboard. We were trotting merrily along the lane that leads to Newfork, thankful in our hearts to be out of the snow,—for there is no snow here. Just ahead of us two little boys were riding along on their ponies. There was a wire fence on both sides of the lane, and almost at the end of the lane an old cow had her head between the wires and was nibbling the tall dead grass. The larger of the two boys said, "That's old Pendry's cow, and she shan't eat a blade of grass off Dad's meadow."

He rode up to the cow and began beating her with his quirt. That frightened the cow, and as she jerked her head up, the top wire caught her across the top of her neck; she jerked and lunged to free herself, and was cruelly cut by the barbs on the wire. Then he began beating his pony.

The small boy said, "You're a coward an' a fool, Billy Polk. The cow wasn't hurtin' nothin', an' you're just tryin' to show off, beatin' that pony."

Said the other boy, "Shut up, you beggar, or I'll beat you; an' I'll take them breeches you got on off you, an' you can go without any— they're mine. My ma give 'em to you."

The little fellow's face was scarlet—as much of it as we could see for the freckles—and his eyes were blazing as he replied, "You ain't man enough. I dare you to strike me or to tech my clothes."

Both boys were riding bareback. The small boy slid off his pony's back; the other rode up to him and raised his quirt, but the little one seized him by the leg, and in a jiffy they were in the road fighting like cats. I asked Mrs. O'Shaughnessy to drive on, but she said, "If you are in a hurry you can try walkin'; I'm goin' to referee this scrap."

It looked for a minute as if the small boy would get a severe beating, but by some trick he hurled the other headlong into the green, slimy water that edged the road; then, seizing the quirt and the opportunity at the same time, he belabored Billy without mercy as that individual climbed up the slippery embankment, blubbering and whipped. Still sobbing, he climbed upon his patient pony, which stood waiting, and galloped off down the lane. The other pony followed and the little conqueror was left afoot.

Mrs. O'Shaughnessy was beaming with delight. "Sure, 'twas a fine fight, a sight worth coming all this way to see. Ah! but you're the b'y. 'Tis a dollar I'd be givin' ye, only me purse is in me stockin'—"

"Oh," the boy said quickly, "don't let that stop you. I'll look off another way."

I don't know if she would have given him the money, for just then some men came into the lane with some cattle and we had to start. The boy got up on the back end of the buckboard and we drove on. We could hear our wagons rumbling along and knew they would soon catch up.

"Where is your home, b'y?" asked Mrs. O'Shaughnessy.

"Oh, just wherever Aunt Hettie has work," he said. "She is at Mr. Tom's now, so I'm there, too,—me and Baby Girl."

"Where are your folks?" Mrs. O'Shaughnessy went on.

"Ma's dead, an' pa's gone to Alasky. I don't know where my brothers are. Baby Girl an' me are with Aunt Het, an' that's all there are of us." He grinned cheerfully in spite of the fact that one eye was fast closing and he bore numerous bumps and scratches on his face and head.

Just then one of the men with the cattle galloped up and shouted, "Hello!" It was Mr. Burney! "Where'd you get that kid? I guess I'll have to get the sheriff after you for kidnapping Bud. And what have you been doing to him, anyway?"

Mrs. O'Shaughnessy entered delightedly into a recital of the "mix-up," and it turned out that Mr. Tom and Mr. Burney were one. It was like meeting an old friend; he seemed as pleased as we and insisted on our going up to his ranch; he said "the missus" would feel slighted if we passed her by. So we turned into another lane, and presently drew up before the ranch house. "The missus" came dancing out to meet us, and right welcome she made us feel. Mr. Burney went back to bring the rest, but they were already setting up the tents and had supper almost ready. However, we stayed and had supper with the Burneys.

They are powerfully happy and talked eagerly of themselves and their prospects. "It's just grand to have a home of your own and some one to do for. I just *love* to mend for Tommy, but I always hated to mend before," said the missus.

"You bet," Mr. Burney answered, "it is sure fine to know there's somebody at home with a pretty pink dress on, waitin' for a fellow when he comes in from a long day in the saddle."

And so they kept up their thoughtless chatter; but every word was as a stab to poor Aunt Hettie. She had Baby Girl on her lap and was giving the children their supper, but I noticed that she ate nothing. It was easy to see that she was not strong. Baby Girl is four years old and is the fattest little thing. She has very dark blue eyes with long, black lashes, and the shortest, most turned-up little nose. She is so plump and rosy that even the faded old blue denim dress could not hide her loveliness.

Mrs. O'Shaughnessy could not keep her eyes off the children. "What is the little girl's name?" she asked.

"Caroline Agnes Lucia Lavina Ida Eunice," was the astonishing reply.

Mrs. O'Shaughnessy gasped. "My *goodness*," she exclaimed; "is that *all?*"

"Oh, no," Aunt Hettie went on placidly; "you see, her mother couldn't call her all the names, so she just used the first letters. They spell Callie; so that is what she called her. But I don't like the name. I call her Baby Girl."

I asked her how she ever came to name her that way, and she said, "My sister wanted a girl, but there were six boys before this little one came. Each time she hoped it would be a girl, and accordingly selected a name for a girl. So there were six names saved up, and as there wasn't much else to give her, my sister gave them *all* to the baby."

After supper the Burneys rode down to camp with us. We had the same camping ground that we had when we came up. The cabin across the creek, where we met Grandma Mortimer, is silent and deserted; the young couple have moved away with their baby.

Mrs. O'Shaughnessy kept talking about the fight, and Mr. Burney gave us the history of the children. "Their mother," he began, "has been dead about eighteen months. She really died with a broken heart. Baby Girl was only a few weeks old when the father went to Alaska, and I guess he's dead. He was to 'a' been back in three years, and no one has ever heard a word from him. His name was Bolton; he was a good fellow, only he went bughouse over the gold fields and just fretted till he got away—sold everything for a grub stake—left his wife and seven kids almost homeless. But they managed some way till the mother died. With her last breath she asked that the two youngest be kept together; she knew the oldest ones would have to be separated. She never did give up looking for Bolton and she wanted him to have the babies.

"Her sister Hettie has worked around here for years; her and Rob Langley have been going to marry ever since I can remember, but always there has something cropped up. And now that Hettie has got to take care of the kids I guess they won't never marry; she won't burden him with them. It is hard for her to support them, too. Work is scarce, and she can't get it, lots of times, because of the kids."

The Burneys soon went home and the rest of us went to bed,—all except Mrs. O'Shaughnessy, who was so cranky and snappy that we left her by the fire. It seemed hours after when I awoke. She was still sitting by the fire; she was absently marking in the ashes with a stick. I happened to be the first one up next morning and as I stirred up the fire I saw "Baby" written in the ashes. We had breakfasted and the men had gone their ways when Mrs. O'Shaughnessy said to me,—

"It is a blessed old soul Mrs. Mortimer is. Do you mind any good lesson that she taught us in the cabin beyont?" I did not remember. "She said, 'The pangs of motherhood make us mothers not only of our own, but of every child that needs mothering,—especially if our own little children need us no longer. Fill their little places with ones who do need us.' Them's her very words, and it's sweet truth it is. Both my Katie and Sheridan have been grown and gone these many years and my heart has ached for childher, and there's none but Cora Belle. I am goin' to get them childher this day. What do you think about it?"

I thought so well of it that in about two minutes we were harnessing the horses and were off to lay the plan before Hettie in record-breaking time.

Poor Hettie: she wept quietly while the advantages of the scheme were being pointed out. She said, "I love the children, dearly, but I am not sure I can always feed and clothe them; that has worried me a lot. I am almost sure Bolton is dead. I'll miss the little things, but I am glad to know they are well provided for. You can take them."

"Now," said Mrs. O'Shaughnessy, "you go on an' marry your man if he is a decent sort. Do it right away before something else happens. It is an illigant wedding present I'll be sendin' you. You must come to see the childher often. What's the b'y's name?"

"We never did name him; you see we had kind of run out of boys' names. We just called him Buddy."

"I can find a name for him," said Mrs. O'Shaughnessy. "Is there a Joseph in the family?" Hettie said no. "Well, then, he is named Joseph Bolton O'Shaughnessy, and I'll have them both baptized as soon as we get to Green River."

So in the morning we start with two new members. Mrs. O'Shaughnessy is very happy. I am so glad myself that I can hardly express myself. We are *all* happy except Mr. Murry; he has at last given up hopes, and gone. Mr. Haynes growls a little about having to travel along with a rolling nursery, but he is just bluffing. I am longing to see Junior. We have not heard one word since we left them, and I am so homesick for mother and my boy. And *you*, best of friends, when shall

I see your beloved face? Tomorrow night we shall camp at Ten Trees and we shall be one day nearer home.

With much love,

Elinore Rupert Stewart.

12

A Stampede

My dear, dear Friend,—

It is with a chastened, humble heart that I begin this letter; I have stood face to face with tragedy and romance, and to me one is as touching as the other, but you will know better when I tell you what I mean. We *all* bustled about to get started from Newfork. Now that we had started, all were homesick. Just ahead of us was a drove of two thousand steers being driven to the railroad to be shipped. I advise you to keep ahead of such drives when you take such a trip, because the trampling of so many feet makes a road almost impassable. What had been snow in the mountains had been rain on the desert, and we found the going decidedly bad. A rise of a hill would give us, now and then, a glimpse of a slow-moving, dark-coloured mass of heaving forms, and the desert breezes brought to our ears the mournful lowing of the poor creatures. Sometimes, too, we could hear a snatch of the cowboys' songs. It was all very beautiful and I would have enjoyed it hugely except that my desire to be home far outran the wagon and I felt like a prisoner with clogs.

We nooned at the cabin of Timothy Hobbs, but no one was at home; he at last had gone "back East" for Jennie. About mid-afternoon the boss of the cow outfit came up on a splendid horse. He was a pleasant fellow and he made a handsome picture, with his big hat, his great chaps and his jangling spurs, as he rode along beside our wagons, talking.

He told us that a crazy duffer had gone about over the desert for years digging wells, but at last he struck water. A few miles ahead was a well flowing like an artesian well. There would be plenty of water for everyone, even the cattle. Next morning we could start ahead of the herds and so the roads would be a little better.

It was quite early when we made camp in the same long draw where we saw Olaf. There was a great change. Where had been dry, burning sand was now a clear little stream that formed shallow pools where the sand had blown away, so that harder soil could form a bottom less greedy than the sand. Off to our left the uneasy herd was being held in a wide, flat valley. They were grazing on the dry, sparse herbage of the desert. Quite near the well the mess-wagon had stopped and the cook was already preparing supper. Beyond, a few yards away, a freighter's long outfit was stopped in the road.

Did you ever see the kind of freight outfit that is used to bring the great loads across the desert? Then I'll tell you about the one we camped near. Freight wagons are not made precisely like others; they are very much larger and stronger. Several of these are coupled together; then as many teams as is necessary are hitched on—making a long, unbroken string of wagons. The horses are arranged in the same manner as the wagons. Great chains are used to pull the wagons, and when a camp is made the whole affair is stopped in the middle of the road and the harness is dropped right where the horse that bore it stood. Many freighters have what they call a coaster hitched to the last wagon. The coaster is almost like other wagons, but it is a home on wheels; it is built and furnished as sheep wagons are. This freighter had one, and as we drove past I was surprised to see the form of a woman and a small boy. We camped quite near them.

For an hour we were very busy preparing supper and arranging for the night. As we sat at supper I thought I had never known so quiet and peaceful an hour. The sun hung like a great, red ball in the hazy west. Purple shadows were already gathering. A gentle wind rippled past across the dun sands and through the gray-green sage.

The chain parts of the hobbles and halters made a clinking sound as the horses fed about. Presently we heard a rumbling just like distant thunder. The cowboys sprang into their saddles; we heard a shot, and then we knew the terrible truth,—the steers had stampeded. For me, the next few minutes were an eternity of frightful confusion. Mrs. O'Shaughnessy and I found ourselves with the children upon our largest wagon; that was absolutely all the protection to be had. It would have gone down like a house of cards if that heaving sea of destruction had turned our way. I was scared witless. Mrs. O'Shaughnessy knelt among the children praying with white lips. I stood up watching the terrible scene. The men hastily set the horses free. There was no time to mount them and ride to safety with so many little children, and as there was nothing to tie them to but the wagons; we *had* to let them go so as to have the wagons left for shelter. *This* is why cowboys are such well-loved figures of romance and in mentioning them romance is fact.

"Greater love hath *no* man than this: that he lay down his life for his brother." They knew nothing about us only that we were defenceless. They rode boldly on their stanch little horses flanking the frenzied steers, shooting a leader here and there as they got a chance. If an animal stumbled it went down to its death, for hundreds of pounding hoofs would trample it to pulp. So it would have been with the boys if their horses had stepped into a badger hole or anything of the kind had happened. So the tide was turned, or the steers kept of themselves, I don't know which, on up the valley instead of coming up our draw. The danger was past.

Presently the cowboys came straggling back. Mrs. O'Shaughnessy ran to meet them. So when two on one horse came with a third riding close beside, helping to hold an injured man on, we knew some one was hurt. Mrs. O'Shaughnessy was, as usual, ready and able to help.

But the freighter's daughter was as quick and had a mattress ready beside the coaster by the time the cowboys came up with the wounded man. Gently the men helped their comrade to the mattress and gently Mrs. O'Shaughnessy and the girl began their work. I quieted the children and put them to bed. The men were busy rounding up the horses. The cowboys kept talking together in low tones and coming and going in twos and threes. They acted so queerly that I wondered if someone else was not hurt. I asked the boss if any more of his men were hurt. He said no, none of *his* men were. I knew none of our men or the freighter were harmed, so I dismissed fear and went to Mrs. O'Shaughnessy.

"Poor boy," she said, "he has a broken thigh and he's hurt inside. His belly is knocked into a cocked-hat. We will pull him through. A man has already gone back to Newfork to get an automobile. They will take him to Rock Springs to the hospital in the morning."

Mrs. O'Shaughnessy and the girl were doing all that could be done; they sent me back to care for the children. To keep warm I crawled under the blankets, but not to sleep. It didn't seem to me that I could *ever* sleep again. I could hear the men talking in subdued tones. The boss was dispatching men to different places. Presently I saw some men take a lantern and move off toward the valley. I could see the light twinkling in and out among the sage-brush. They stopped. I could see forms pass before the light. I wondered what could be the matter. The horses were all safe; even Boy, Mr. Haynes's dog, was safe, shivering and whining on his master's blankets. I could plainly hear the hiccoughs of the wounded man: the click-cluck, click-cluck, kept on with maddening persistence, but at last his nurses forced enough hot water down him to cause vomiting. The blood-clots came and the poor fellow fell asleep. A lantern was hung upon the wagon and the two women went into the coaster to make some coffee.

It was three o'clock in the morning when the men of our outfit came back. They put on their heavy coats and were seeing to their horses. I asked Clyde what was the matter.

"Hush," he said; "lie still. It is Olaf."

"But I want to help," I said.

"You can't help. It's—all over," he replied as he started again to where the lantern was gleaming like a star fallen among the sage.

I tucked the children in a little more snugly, then went over to the coaster.

"Won't you come to bed and rest?" I asked Mrs. O'Shaughnessy.

"No, I'll not. Are me children covered and warm?"

"Yes," I answered.

"What are them fellys pow-wowing about down in the sage?"

"Olaf is dead," I said.

"Who says God is not merciful? Now all the poor felly's troubles are done with. 'Twas him that caused the stampede, mayhap. God send him peace. I am glad. He will never be hungry nor cold any more."

"Yes," said the girl; speaking slowly. "I am glad, too. He almost lived in this draw. We saw him every trip and he *did* suffer. Dad left a little for him to eat and whatever he could to wear every trip. The sheep-herders helped him, too. But he suffered. All the home he had was an old, thrown-away sheep wagon down beyond the last ridge toward the valley. I've seen him every two weeks for ten years. It's a wonder he has not been killed before."

"I wonder," said Mrs. O'Shaughnessy, "if he has any family. Where will they bury him?"

"He has no people. If they will listen to Dad, they will lay him here on the desert. He would want it so."

After breakfast Mrs. O'Shaughnessy lay down for a little rest. When the wounded man awoke the girl gave him a little coffee.

"You're awful good to me," he said. "I'd like to have you around all the time."

The girl smiled gravely. "Ain't you got nobody to take care of you?"

"No. What is your name?"

"Amy Winters. Now you must hush. Talkin' might make you worse."

"I'm not so tur'ble bad off. Where do you live?"

"In the coaster, somewhere on the road between Pinedale and Rock Springs. Dad is a freighter."

"Huh! Do you like to live that way?"

"No; I want a house and a garden awful bad, but Dad can't do nothin' but freight and we've got Jessie to raise. We ain't got no ma."

"Do women *have* to change their names when they marry?"

"I don't know. Reckon they do, though. Why?"

"'Cause my name is Tod Winters. I know where there is a dandy little place up on the Gros Ventre where a cabin would look mighty good to me if there was some one to keep it for me—"

"Oh, say," she interrupted, "that is a awful pretty handkerchief you've got around your neck."

Just then the automobile came up frightening our horses. I heard no more, but the "awful pretty handkerchief" was missing when the hero left for the hospital. They used some lumber from a load the freighter had and walled up a grave for Olaf. They had no tools but axes and a shovel we had along. By noon Olaf was buried. Glenholdt set a slab of sandstone at the head. With his knife he had dug out these words—"Olaf. The friend of horses."

We camped last night at Ten Trees. Tonight we are at Eden Valley. The mystery of Mrs. O'Shaughnessy's sudden change about the license is explained. She unloaded an elk at the Sanders cabin. "'Twas two I aimed to bring you, but me own family has increased by twins whilst I've been gone, so one ilk will have to do you."

So now, dear friend, I am a little nearer you. In one more week I shall be home.

Sincerely, *thankfully* yours,

E. R. S.

13

Nearing Home

At the Well in the Desert,
October 21.

Dear Friend,—

We shall reach Green River City tonight. We will rest the teams one day, then start home. It will take us two days from Green River to reach home, so this is the last letter on the road. When we made camp here last night we saw someone coming on horseback along the *cañon* rim on the opposite side. The form seemed familiar and the horse looked like one I had seen, but I dared not believe my eyes. Clyde, who was helping to draw water from the eighty-foot well without a pulley, thought I was bereft as I ran from the camp toward the advancing rider. But although I thought what I saw must be a mirage, still I knew Mrs. Louderer on Bismarck.

Out of breath from my run, I grasped her fat ankle and panted till I could speak.

"Haf they run you out of camp, you iss so bad?" she asked me by way of greeting. Then, more kindly, "Your boy iss all right, the mutter also. I am come, though, to find you. It iss time you are home with the *kinder*. Haf you any goose-grease left?"

I had, all she had given me.

At camp, joy knew no bounds. Never was one more welcome than our beloved neighbour. Her astonishment knew no bounds either, when her big blue eyes rested upon Mrs. O'Shaughnessy's "twins."

"Frau O'Shaughnessy," she said severely, "what have you here? You iss robbed an orphan asylum. How haf you come by these?"

Mrs. O'Shaughnessy is so full of life and good spirits and so delighted to talk about her "childher" that she gave a very animated recital of how she became a happy mother. In turn Mrs. Louderer told how she grew more and more alarmed by our long absence, but decided not to alarm the neighbours, so she had "made a search party out of mineself," and had fared forth to learn our fate.

We had a merry supper; even Haynes became cheerful, and there was no lagging next morning when we started for home. When people go on elk hunts they are very likely to return in tatters, so I am going to leave it to your imagination to picture our appearance when we drove up to the rear of the hotel about sundown. Our friend Mrs. Hutton came running to meet us. I was ashamed to go into her house, but she leaned up against the house and laughed until tears came. "*What* chased you?" she gasped. "You must have been run through some of those barbed wire things that they are putting up to stop the German army."

Mrs. Hutton is a little lady who bolsters up self-respect and makes light of trying situations, so she "shooed" us in and I sneaked into my room and waited until Clyde could run down to the store and purchase me a dress. I feel quite clean and respectable now, sitting up here in my room writing this to you. I will soon be at home now. Until then goodbye.

E. R. S.

14

The Memory-Bed

Dear, Dear Friend,—

Can you guess how happy I am? *Be it ever so humble there is no place like home.*

It is so good to sit in my creaky old rocker, to hold Junior, to feel his dear weight; to look at my brave little mother. I do not like the "in-law." She is *mother* to me. Under the east window of our dining-room we have a flower-bed. We call it our memory-bed because Clyde's first wife had it made and kept pansies growing there. We poured the water of my little lost boy's last bath onto the memory-bed. I keep pansies growing in one side of the bed in memory of her who loved them. In the other end I plant sweet alyssum in memory of my baby. A few pansies and a tuft of sweet alyssum smiled a welcome, though all the rest of my flowers were dead. We have a hop-vine at the window and it has protected the flowers in the memory-bed. How happy I have been, looking over the place! Some young calves have come while we were gone; a whole squirming nest full of little pigs. My chickens have outgrown my knowledge.

There is no snow here at all. Our experiences on our trip seem almost unreal, but the wagon-load of meat to be attended to is a reminder of realities. I have had a fine trip; I have experienced about all the human emotions. I had not expected to encounter so many people or to get the little inside glimpses that I've had, but wherever there are human beings there are the little histories. I have come home realizing anew how happy I am, how much I have been spared, and how many of life's blessings are mine. Poor Mrs. Louderer, childless and alone, openly envying Mrs. O'Shaughnessy her babies! In my bedroom there is a row of four little brown heads asleep on their pillows. Four precious kiddies all my own. And not the least of my blessings, *you* to tell my happiness to. Has my trip interested you, dear friend? I *hope* you liked it. It will lose a little of its charm for me if you find it uninteresting.

I will write you again soon.

Your happy friend,

E. R. S.

LEONAUR

ALSO FROM LEONAUR
AVAILABLE IN SOFTCOVER OR HARDCOVER WITH DUST JACKET

A DIARY FROM DIXIE *by Mary Boykin Chesnut*—A Lady's Account of the Confederacy During the American Civil War

FOLLOWING THE DRUM *by Teresa Griffin Vielé*—A U. S. Infantry Officer's Wife on the Texas frontier in the Early 1850's

FOLLOWING THE GUIDON *by Elizabeth B. Custer*—The Experiences of General Custer's Wife with the U. S. 7th Cavalry.

LADIES OF LUCKNOW *by G. Harris & Adelaide Case*—The Experiences of Two British Women During the Indian Mutiny 1857. A Lady's Diary of the Siege of Lucknow by G. Harris, Day by Day at Lucknow by Adelaide Case

MARIE-LOUISE AND THE INVASION OF 1814 *by Imbert de Saint-Amand*—The Empress and the Fall of the First Empire

SAPPER DOROTHY *by Dorothy Lawrence*—The only English Woman Soldier in the Royal Engineers 51st Division, 79th Tunnelling Co. during the First World War

ARMY LETTERS FROM AN OFFICER'S WIFE 1871-1888 *by Frances M. A. Roe*—Experiences On the Western Frontier With the United States Army

NAPOLEON'S LETTERS TO JOSEPHINE *by Henry Foljambe Hall*—Correspondence of War, Politics, Family and Love 1796-1814

MEMOIRS OF SARAH DUCHESS OF MARLBOROUGH, AND OF THE COURT OF QUEEN ANNE VOLUME 1 by A. T. Thomson

MEMOIRS OF SARAH DUCHESS OF MARLBOROUGH, AND OF THE COURT OF QUEEN ANNE VOLUME 2 by A. T. Thomson

MARY PORTER GAMEWELL AND THE SIEGE OF PEKING *by A. H. Tuttle*—An American Lady's Experiences of the Boxer Uprising, China 1900

VANISHING ARIZONA *by Martha Summerhayes*—A young wife of an officer of the U.S. 8th Infantry in Apacheria during the 1870's

THE RIFLEMAN'S WIFE *by Mrs. Fitz Maurice*—*The Experiences of an Officer's Wife and Chronicles of the Old 95th During the Napoleonic Wars*

THE OATMAN GIRLS *by Royal B. Stratton*—The Capture & Captivity of Two Young American Women in the 1850's by the Apache Indians

LEONAUR

ALSO FROM LEONAUR

AVAILABLE IN SOFTCOVER OR HARDCOVER WITH DUST JACKET

THE WOMAN IN BATTLE by Loreta Janeta Velazquez—Soldier, Spy and Secret Service Agent for the Confederacy During the American Civil War.

BOOTS AND SADDLES by Elizabeth B. Custer—The experiences of General Custer's Wife on the Western Plains.

FANNIE BEERS' CIVIL WAR by Fannie A. Beers—A Confederate Lady's Experiences of Nursing During the Campaigns & Battles of the American Civil War.

LADY SALE'S AFGHANISTAN by Florentia Sale—An Indomitable Victorian Lady's Account of the Retreat from Kabul During the First Afghan War.

THE TWO WARS OF MRS DUBERLY by Frances Isabella Duberly—An Intrepid Victorian Lady's Experience of the Crimea and Indian Mutiny.

THE REBELLIOUS DUCHESS by Paul F. S. Dermoncourt—The Adventures of the Duchess of Berri and Her Attempt to Overthrow French Monarchy.

LADIES OF WATERLOO by Charlotte A. Eaton, Magdalene de Lancey & Juana Smith—The Experiences of Three Women During the Campaign of 1815: Waterloo Days by Charlotte A. Eaton, A Week at Waterloo by Magdalene de Lancey & Juana's Story by Juana Smith.

NURSE AND SPY IN THE UNION ARMY by Sarah Emma Evelyn Edmonds—During the American Civil War

WIFE NO. 19 by Ann Eliza Young—The Life & Ordeals of a Mormon Woman During the 19th Century

DIARY OF A NURSE IN SOUTH AFRICA by Alice Bron—With the Dutch-Belgian Red Cross During the Boer War

MARIE ANTOINETTE AND THE DOWNFALL OF ROYALTY by Imbert de Saint-Amand—The Queen of France and the French Revolution

THE MEMSAHIB & THE MUTINY by R. M. Coopland—An English lady's ordeals in Gwalior and Agra duringthe Indian Mutiny 1857

MY CAPTIVITY AMONG THE SIOUX INDIANS by Fanny Kelly—The ordeal of a pioneer woman crossing the Western Plains in 1864

WITH MAXIMILIAN IN MEXICO by Sara Yorke Stevenson—A Lady's experience of the French Adventure

LEONAUR

ALSO FROM LEONAUR
AVAILABLE IN SOFTCOVER OR HARDCOVER WITH DUST JACKET

PLAINS WOMEN *by Lydia Spencer Lane & Lodisa Frizzell*—Two accounts of American Women on the Western Frontier. I Married a Soldier or Old Days in the Old Army by Lydia Spencer Lane, Across the Plains to California in 1852 Journal of Mrs. Lodisa Frizzell by Lodisa Frizzell

THE WHITE SLAVE MARKET*by Mrs. Archibald Mackirdy (Olive Christian Malvery) and William Nicholas Willis*—An Overview of the Traffic in Young Women at the Turn of the Nineteenth and Early Twentieth Centuries

"TELL IT ALL" *by Fanny Stenhouse*—The Ordeals of a Woman Against Polygamy Within the Mormon Church During the 19th Century

TENTING ON THE PLAINS *by Elizabeth B. Custer*—The Experiences of General Custer's Wife in Kansas and Texas.

CAPTIVES! *by Cynthia Ann Parker, Mrs Jannette E. De Camp Sweet, Mary Schwandt, Mrs. Caroline Harris, Misses Frances and Almira Hall & Nancy McClure*—The Narratives of Seven Women Taken Prisoner by the Plains Indians of the American West

FRIENDS AND FOES IN THE TRANSKEI *by Helen M. Prichard*—A Victorian lady's experience of Southern Africa during the 1870's

NURSE EDITH CAVELL *by William Thomson Hill & Jacqueline Van Til*—Two accounts of a Notable British Nurse of the First World War. The Martyrdom of Nurse Cavell by William Thompson Hill, With Edith Cavell by Jacqueline Van Til

PERSONAL RECOLLECTIONS OF JOAN OF ARC *by Mark Twain*

FIELD HOSPITAL AND FLYING COLUMN *by Violetta Thurstan*—With the Red Cross on the Western & Eastern Fronts During the First World War.

THE CELLAR-HOUSE OF PERVYSE *by G. E. Mitton*—The Incredible Account of Two Nurses on the Western Front During the Great War.

A WOMAN'S EXPERIENCES IN THE GREAT WAR *by Louise Mack*—An Australian Author's Clandestine Journey Through War-Torn Belgium.

THE LOVE LETTERS OF HENRY VIII TO ANNE BOLEYN & OTHER CORRESPONDENCE & DOCUMENTS CONCERNING HENRY AND HIS WIVES *by Henry VIII and Henry Ellis*

A LADY'S CAPTIVITY AMONG CHINESE PIRATES *by Fanny Loviot*—The Adventures of a Lady Traveller During the 1850s